DRESSING
the
RESISTANCE

DRESSING
the
RESISTANCE

The
Visual Language
of Protest
Through History

Camille Benda

Foreword by Ane Crabtree

Princeton Architectural Press · New York

Published by
Princeton Architectural Press
202 Warren Street
Hudson, New York 12534
www.papress.com

Printed and bound in Singapore
25 24 23 22 4 3 2 1 First edition

ISBN 978-1-61689-988-2

Every reasonable attempt has been made to identify owners of copyright.
Errors or omissions will be corrected in subsequent editions.

Editor: Kristen Hewitt
Designer: Natalie Snodgrass

Library of Congress Control Number: 2021935513

COVER IMAGE CREDITS
Front cover: Reuters/Edgard Garrido/Alamy Stock Photo, p. 116 (top left); Keystone
Press / Alamy Stock Photo, p. 84 (top right); Joerg Boethling/Alamy Stock Photo, p. 106
(bottom left); Reuters/Lucas Jackson, p. 203 (bottom right)
Back cover: Imperial War Museum, London, IWM Non Commercial License, p. 150

CONTENTS

Foreword

There has never been a more defining time for *Dressing the Resistance*. As I write this, six Asian women have been murdered in Atlanta by a young white male who was "having a bad day." Xenophobic violence against Asian and Black Americans shows no sign of slowing, women's abortion rights look like something out of the Dark Ages, and through it all, people are coming together in a collective show of solidarity. The world feels lit up like a powder keg, and within these protests are the uniforms of opposition, dissent, and outcry worn by the very people fighting for their lives.

Throughout history, clothing has lent the wearer power by allowing them to express rage, anger, unfathomable sorrow, spirituality, cultural connection, political affiliation, and outbursts of pure joy—especially when the wearer wasn't at liberty to verbalize their true thoughts. At times clothing has been a means of amplifying our voices and feelings to a higher state of expression.

When asked to write this, I hesitated. Then the memories of the past four years came flooding back, not just of the former president of the United States that I refuse to mention by name, but the very personal work I was doing as costume designer for *The Handmaid's Tale*. The concept was simple: create a uniform for "every woman," of every glorious shape and size. The color red is rooted in women's menses and the lifeblood that flows through us all.

For me, the show mirrored a life of personal protest: The abortion clinics visited out of necessity in the 1980s in New York City, the marches to protest the murder of Amadou Diallo, the Free Mumia movement, my research into the Wounded Knee Occupation, and more. Life mirroring art mirroring life happened seamlessly after that handmaid's costume, moving beyond the parameters of Atwood's book into protests in Poland, Brazil, Argentina, the United States, and elsewhere—women standing together for women's rights. Humbling, to be sure.

This is a book that we will remember as a virtual bookmark for political declaration, not just for one group but for many. Whether dressing as an individual or collectively, the body as real estate elevates clothing as an integral part of protest and intent. This is something that artists have done since time immemorial. Art is not frivolous. It can state things that we cannot say aloud. It is our ephemeral voice.

Dressing the Resistance reveals that across all races, cultures, and personal histories, we are all fighting the same fight. It influences us to "take up our arms" (our voices) and demand, through clothing and costume, "What will you do to join the resistance?"

—Ane Crabtree, March 2021

Preface

"We all have a memoir in miniature living in a garment we've worn."
—*Emily Spivack*, Worn Stories, *2014*

My perspective on protest, resistance, and personal freedom is rooted in a global turmoil made intensely personal. My parents were refugees who left Czechoslovakia during the communist occupation. They escaped to the United States in 1968, after the Prague Spring, not knowing if or when they would return to live in their home country again. They never did, and after claiming asylum in the United States, it was years before they saw their families again.

Wrapped up in this sort of dual nationality, I grew up as both Czech and American, code-switching between the two. Notions of personal identity, belonging, and otherness are all concepts that are visually encoded in clothing, fashion, and costume. No surprise, then, that I became fascinated with how individuals express themselves to the world. Objects and clothing became precious records of my own family history. One year, my grandmother sent us a pair of garnet earrings, hand-sewn into the dress fabric of a traditional Czechoslovak doll, her way of sneaking a family heirloom out of the communist state. Rather than a whole jewelry box handed down to me, those earrings and the doll were some of the only survivors of my grandmother's belongings, the rest left behind.

When my parents were finally able to travel after gaining their American citizenship when I was seven, they brought me to visit the country they grew up in. There was no way to explain to a kid who grew up in an American suburb with bountiful grocery stores that even a single orange was precious in Czechoslovakia! Later, as a young adult, I'd sit in a Prague beer hall with Czech friends and compare our lives and opportunities, thrilled that I could drink beer at eighteen. My parents' friends were activists, theater directors, and artists, so I learned by osmosis how powerful covert rebellion through art and design could be.

It wasn't all serious though. The irony was lost on me when I stomped through my grandmother's Moravian village in 1985, a teenage goth in layers of black, my hair dyed in three colors, rebelling against nothing, while the resistance to communism ramped up in Czechoslovak cities. When communism fell in 1989, my family and I were there for New Year's Eve, tearing political posters off the walls to take home as souvenirs. My love of wild clothing and adornment as a fifteen-year-old grew into a passion for costume design and dress history, probably because clothes are such a powerful vessel for emotion, self-expression, and memory. The garments in this book tell the story of people, ordinary and extraordinary, whose lives were caught in revolution, cultural change, and turmoil.

Clothing as Canvas

"Every revolution begins with a change of clothes."

—René Bizet, French journalist and critic, 1913

Fashion, clothing, textiles, accessories, and costume have served a critical role in protest movements throughout history. Clothing often offers the most basic opportunity for groups to rebel: a simple, mundane item that can symbolize discontent. British punks took the humble safety pin from the household sewing kit, punched it through an earlobe, and headed out to face a bleak 1970s postwar world in which they had no voice. Male farmers in rural India wore their wives' saris while staging sit-ins on railroad tracks against government neglect. American suffragettes made and wore dresses from old newspapers printed with pro-voting slogans.

During the LA Riots in 1992, protesters painted, ripped, or stenciled their T-shirts, using clothing as a canvas to create community around their rebellion. Los Angeles college student and Navy veteran Mark Craig threw on a T-shirt during a night of civil disobedience that ended up with him grabbing the national spotlight on the cover of *Newsweek*. His T-shirt was displayed in the California African American Museum as part of an LA Riots retrospective: the object (T-shirt) plus the meaning (social discontent) combine to create a historical artifact with a legacy. [Fig.1] Clothing can carry emotions and memories, as Shahidha Bari notes in her book *Dressed: A Philosophy of Clothes* (2020): "Sometimes, there is, in dress, only anguish: the garments that bring to you the memory of someone you once loved and will never see again, the bloodstain on a T-shirt from that most terrible of days."[1] It is indeed powerful to see the LA Riots T-shirt on the cover of *Newsweek*, but to see the T-shirt in person in a museum, with all its holes and imperfections, induces goose bumps.

Clothing provides a compelling canvas for registering rebellion: a super visual, universal, portable cue that can be photographed, distributed, copied, and built on by future protesters across languages and cultures. When the Trump administration came to power in the United States, protests reverberated worldwide. During the four years that Donald Trump held office, it seemed that each day brought a new image gone viral: of the Women's Marches, the Black Lives Matter demonstrations, the #MeToo movement, the Gilets Jaunes demonstrations in France, Kamala Harris wearing all white for her vice presidential acceptance speech, anti-Brexit protesters holding satirical puppets of politicians, citizens in Hong Kong marching under a sea of yellow umbrellas, Nigerian activists rallying against

Fig.1
Mark Craig (left), Rodney King protests,
Los Angeles, 1992

police violence. Protest has once again entered the zeitgeist.
And as long as there have been protest movements, citizens,
activists, and freedom fighters have used art and design to
amplify, elevate, articulate, and define their causes.

Just hats alone can tell the story of design and material
culture—many are dotted throughout this book, from the
iconic Black Panthers' beret to Gandhi's humble topi hat, from
Caribbean rebel headwraps to French World War II protest
millinery. In 2016, Jayna Zweiman and Krista Suh launched
the Pussyhat Project, and the soft knitted pink pussyhats went
head-to-head with cardinal-red MAGA baseball caps reading
"MAKE AMERICA GREAT AGAIN" in white embroidery. [Fig.3]
The year 2017 brought the crisp white bonnet from the hit TV
show *The Handmaid's Tale*, worn by activists as an homage

to the original costumes designed by Ane Crabtree. [Fig.2] The #MeToo movement celebrated the handmaid costumes, with activists buying versions of the costume online or making them at home, and took to the city streets and government buildings donning the eerie red dresses and white bonnets. The costumes were endlessly photographed and viscerally haunting. In 1951, art historian Quentin Bell wrote an article called "The Incorrigible Habit." He forever tied phenomena like *The Handmaid's Tale* costumes to activism and clothing: "The history of dress is, to a very large extent, a history of protests."[2]

While the handmaid protesters wore custom dresses and bonnets, the MAGA hat was a factory-made, synthetic-dyed symbol of American masculinity and national sport in the form of the baseball hat. In his 2015 *New York Times Magazine* article on the history of the baseball cap, writer Troy Patterson concludes, "The hat is not a fashion item, it's something larger, and more primal: the headpiece of American folk costume."[3] The baseball cap started as sports uniform but became a symbol of the common American citizen. Trump's marketing team took it to another level when they propelled such a humble accessory into political history.

Global unrest and protests around equity and justice, triggered by the Trump administration but already brewing long beforehand, bring up daily debate about free speech, hate speech, and freedom of expression. How do activists, dissenters, and agitators make their voices heard without silencing the voices of others? How do we as an international world community of vastly different rules, resources, and requirements hold space for each individual view? American writer and cultural critic James Baldwin observed that art, design, and craft could be our ally in striving to understand the society around us and the myriad opinions we all hold. He was interviewed for *Life* magazine in 1963, but his words are as compelling today. Baldwin assigns a profound role to art: "An artist is a sort of emotional or spiritual historian. His role is to make you realize the doom and glory of knowing who you are and what you are."[4]

The following chapters document and decode the living history of dress and resistance. For anyone trying to make sense of our turbulent times, design can be a guide, reflecting our world back at us, uncovering deeper meanings, transforming words and thoughts into visuals. Through photographs, art, engravings, painting, and sculpture, we can see dress as a

Fig.2
Handmaid protester, Brett Kavanaugh
confirmation hearings, September 4, 2018

visually engaging and historically compelling exploration of
many types of rebellion: formalized protests; civil disobedience; peaceful and violent uprisings; informal, impromptu, and
covert resistance. Social activism, sit-ins, flash mobs, boycotts,
street theater, and industrial action all reveal ways in which we
use protest in the service of progress and change.

Although different countries use protest in unique ways,
protests across time periods reveal that the human need to be
heard is centuries old and also utterly current. Crucial, pivotal
movements for Indigenous rights, civil rights, climate change
awareness, pay equity, women's rights, gender equality, and
disability rights have altered the course of society. A protester
sacrifices their safety and personal freedom to rebel—and on
their backs are the clothes that will become symbols of the
revolution. These tools have served as markers in time, documenting the ephemeral moments of movements, cementing
them in history for future generations.

Universal themes run deep through the history of dress—
subversion, conformity, imitation, confrontation, uniformity,
appropriation, shock, nudity, fear, and parody—and provide
common ground for all human expression. Creating new fashions or distinctive garments and accessories has given dissenters of all nations a strong nonverbal tool, the mass use of which

Fig.3
MAGA supporter, Alabama state
elections, September 7, 2018

creates a powerful repeated image that can lodge in the minds
of the public. Activists have used the whole spectrum of fashion, whether everyday dress and accessories, haute couture, or
avant-garde dress, to further their causes. Costume and performance can be crucial tools for enhancing visibility for a cause.
And finally, removing clothing as an act of protest can be as
compelling as completely covering oneself.

In this book, every individual story matters. Cultures
throughout history have used clothing, accessories, and costumes as a catalyst in the struggle for social change, and regular,
everyday people have harnessed this visual power to heighten
their message. The following chapters celebrate diverse freedom fighters from across the planet and throughout human
history. Abolitionist and Underground Railroad hero Harriet
Tubman, born in 1822, came from enslaved origins, but her
clothing tells stories just as momentous as those of Louis XIV,
the eighteenth-century king of France. Tubman wore humble, utilitarian clothes as she guided slaves to freedom—men's
overcoats, sturdy wool hats, hobnail boots. In stark contrast,
Louis XIV, sometimes called Louis Couture, was known for his
ferocious love of the finest clothes, accessories, wigs, and jewels
available. He famously gave clothing one of its biggest compli-
ments, declaring that "fashion is the mirror of history."

PART ONE

Status,
Class, Dress

CHAPTER 1

Power to the People: Everyday Dress as Protest

"Protest is the yes to the rights of the powerless, the oppressed, and the marginalized."

—*From* Protest: The Aesthetics of Resistance, *Zurich University for the Arts, Exhibition Catalog, 2018*

The powerless, the oppressed, and the marginalized have, throughout history, transformed the clothes on their backs into symbols of dissent. Ordinary dress is the visual voice of common people: simple clothes have complex meanings. Typically, members of society who hold the most resources have the loudest voices, and communities with the least resources must shout to be heard. The working classes have often used the little they have to kick off social change by making choices that convey a clear message. Clothing, art, and design help underrepresented groups—when they grab a T-shirt, write a slogan, develop an emblem, or reclaim a symbol of oppression—shout and be heard. What begins as a grassroots motif (like the Black Power fist) can end up as a triumph of graphic design that inspires future generations.

In documentary photographs, news footage, and social media, protesters frequently use staples of our modern Western wardrobe—garments like jeans, T-shirts, overalls, coveralls, leather boots, baseball hats, and bandanas—as protest gear. If you start looking for clues in clothing, you can begin to recognize the origins of social history in almost every item of dress. The brave generations before us, who ignited change through the clothes they wore, have inspired trends that are reflected in the fashion we wear today. Your pair of plain blue jeans are not just a simple wardrobe staple but a visual nod to working-class American immigrants who wore them a century ago.

Similarly, traditional dress from around the globe, along with folk costume and peasant clothing—Indian saris, Native American deerskin shirts, traditional African textile prints—can elevate a message of collective action. Cultures can use traditional dress to celebrate heritage, commemorate national values, and inspire patriotism. This makes it a potent tool for rebels. Traditional dress and everyday Western dress are records of human culture, and protesters can subvert, reclaim, reframe, and invent new clothing styles to reflect cultural shifts and changes.

The woman in *The Gardener*, by artists and community activists John Ahearn and Rigoberto Torres, is Melissa, whose face they immortalized in a plaster life cast for their 1979 project South Bronx Hall of Fame. [Fig.1] In capturing the faces of the local community around them, they made the mundane otherworldly. When translated into sculpture, Melissa's tools of the trade and her simple, functional clothes—a bright red Bob Marley sweatshirt, itself a symbol of rebel spirit, plain white canvas pants, and worn blue tennis shoes—become symbols of the working classes.

19

Visibility is key in activism for groups that have been traditionally underrepresented in art and design, and through their art, Ahearn and Torres give voice to a woman who may not have otherwise been truly seen.

Humble, durable, and instantly recognizable, the denim overall has for two hundred years symbolized hard toil in fields and factories. In the 1960s, the American civil rights movement reclaimed this garment, one that held memories of enslavement, and lifted it up as a symbol of resistance. Black activists from all socioeconomic classes wore overalls to protests: the middle classes proudly took on this worker's uniform to show solidarity, while the younger generations wore the garments of their grandparents to honor their heritage. Earlier, in the 1920s, American citizens, protesting the high cost of living, formed "overalls clubs." Going through daily life dressed in denim coveralls, pants, and jackets (and as rumor has it, going out to dinner and even getting married in them) gave ordinary people a visual way to signal their discontent.

A 1964 poster for the Student Nonviolent Coordinating Committee, a civil rights group, shows an older Black man in a straw farm hat, short-sleeved work shirt, dusty, beaten leather boots, and well-worn overalls. [Fig.2] Known as SNCC, the grassroots organization became one of the most prominent forces in the civil rights movement. Photographer Danny Lyon, the first staff photographer for SNCC, propelled overalls into the cultural consciousness with this black-and-white snapshot. In a 2013 article for the *Journal of Southern History*, author, professor, and fashion historian Tanisha C. Ford coined the term "SNCC skin"[1] referring to the stylized, symbolic uniform of overalls, denim, and natural Black hair that SNCC women wore during marches, demonstrations, and rallies. Poignantly, the word "skin" gives the SNCC uniform layers of meaning: it references Black skin, of course, and also an outer metaphorical skin, unifying the activists through dress.

Denim innovation skyrocketed in nineteenth-century America as miners, railroad workers, former slaves, and farmers became Levi Strauss's first customers, but denim technology originated with eighteenth-century French work wear. Durable cotton textile weaving and cheap indigo-blue dye made manual laborers easily identifiable in rural France, and the uniform eventually spread across Europe, Australia, New Zealand, South Africa, and North America in the nineteenth century. While Levi Strauss & Co. might be the most famous global denim brand, there were hundreds of immigrant Jewish tailors and fabric merchants in San Francisco

Fig. 1 (opposite)
The Gardener (Melissa with Bob Marley shirt) by John Ahearn and Rigoberto Torres, 1997/2007

One Man
One Vote

STUDENT NONVIOLENT COORDINATING COMMITTEE
8½ RAYMOND STREET, N.W. ATLANTA 14, GEORGIA

Lincoln Lithograph Company

Danny Lyon

Fig.5
"Jane Fonda for President" T-shirt,
FIDM Museum Collection, 1970–75

and New York who brought their skills after fleeing religious oppression in Eastern Europe. Overalls rapidly evolved to fill the needs of workers, resulting in sturdy rivets for pocket reinforcement and belt loops for gold miners who refused to wear suspenders because they got caught on machinery in the mines. In short, one of America's iconic fashion contributions was pioneered by foreigners seeking refuge from political persecution.

In 2019 Miko Underwood launched her sustainable denim brand Oak & Acorn, revisiting the heritage of overalls in its newest collection. [Fig.3] Underwood is passionate about equity in fashion, manufacturing her gender-neutral collection in Harlem, New York. Tying her collection directly to fashion and activism, she describes how "the depiction of models Gerald, Mekahel, and Shauna in the image is a reenactment of how members of the Student Non-Violent Coordinating Committee of the 1960s American civil rights movement wore denim as an act of camaraderie, protection, functionality, and protest.[2] The Denim Collective, Underwood's

Fig.6
Water contamination protests, Detroit, Michigan, March 3, 2016

educational initiative, takes activism a step further with this manifesto demanding "the documentation of historical truths, the right of visual representation and the right to be recognized justly."[3]

A 2002 advertising campaign for the Italian brand Rifle sold denim and social commentary simultaneously. Slovenian Tomato Košir photographed a pair of faded blue jeans on a white background, one leg tied in a knot. The campaign was called "War Wear Rifle," and the image is a commentary on soldiers returning from battle. The tied knot in the pants leg chillingly alludes to a limb lost in combat. [Fig.4]

The history of the T-shirt (a steadfast style companion to denim jeans) is the history of the working classes. Originally worn by soldiers as a washable cotton underlayer, T-shirts seeped into casual Western dress as early twentieth-century sportswear and then through post–World War II youth culture. When used as a tool for protesting, the T-shirt becomes a walking billboard—front and back, you can print on it, paint on it, shred it, chop it, and write whatever message you want on it. In the collection of the Fashion Institute of Design and Merchandising (FIDM) Museum in Los Angeles, a "Jane Fonda for President" T-shirt lays in an archival box of tissue paper. [Fig.5] This plain, utilitarian piece of clothing becomes a tongue-in-cheek historical record of Fonda's long and controversial life as an activist. Fonda started as an actress and activist in the 1960s and became a fitness guru in the 1980s; and at eighty-one years old in 2019, Fonda started Fire Drill Fridays, wearing a stylish red coat and picketing against climate change in front of the White House, getting repeatedly and publicly arrested by Washington, DC, police.

In a 2016 news photograph, activists in Detroit, Michigan, stand in a snowy city street outside the Republican presidential candidates debate to bring awareness to the water crisis in Flint, where systemic racism has affected working-class Flint residents disproportionally, especially people of color. [Fig.6] The muted tones, canvas work wear, T-shirts, jeans, beanie hats, and leather jackets form a tableau of blue-collar clothing. The unifying power of common, ordinary clothes like these has been harnessed in movements around the world.

The spontaneous marches after George Floyd's killing in 2020 propelled an informal Facebook group of moms in Portland to dig into their garages for construction masks, bike helmets, and safety goggles; grab any piece of yellow clothing from their closets; and link arms to form a wall supporting Black Lives Matter protesters.

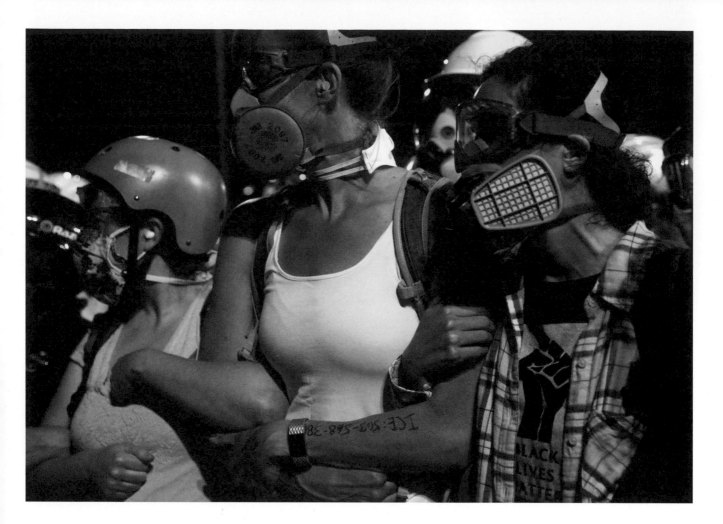

The viral images exploded across social media. Color, mundane household objects, and women's bodies created instant branding and publicity for the movement. [**Fig.7**]

Almost anything portable and paintable can become a canvas when you're starting a rebellion. During the 2014 Revolution of Dignity in Ukraine, antigovernment protesters hand painted hard hats with political slogans, decorations, and folk art. The effect was beautiful and functional, and the hats became lasting symbols of the event. [**Fig.8**] Some forty years earlier, the Hard Hat Riot raged in New York City, when unions encouraged construction work-ers to clash with Vietnam War protesters. Weeks later, President Richard Nixon invited the construction workers to the White House for a discussion, and a photo op immortalized the many customized hard hats that the protesters had made. [**Fig.9**]

While everyday garments exist firmly in the mundane moments of our lives, fashion and haute couture revels in imag-ining alternate worlds. But a poetic juxtaposition happened in France during the 2019 Gilets Jaunes (yellow vests) demonstrations against the high cost of living and fuel prices. [**Fig.10**] European

Fig.7 (above)
"Portland Moms" protest group, Portland, Oregon, July 24, 2020

Fig. 8 (left top)
Painted protest helmets, Ukraine, 2014

Fig. 9 (left bottom)
Hard Hat Riot helmets, the White House, Washington, DC, May 26, 1970

Fig. 10 (right)
Gilets Jaunes protests, Nice, France, January 12, 2019

road rules require all cars to have a safety kit on board, complete with a yellow high-visibility vest; anyone can pull one out of their trunk, grab a marker, and use it as a billboard, writing on the back surface. That same year, during the events of the high-profile Paris Fashion Week, a long-haired man wore an oversized, six-foot-tall haute couture version of the Gilet Jaune. Made from screaming neon neoprene and safety tape, the clash of fashion and work wear amplified the Gilets Jaunes mass movement, transforming the vest from a utilitarian piece of safety equipment into avant-garde commentary.

Similarly, fine art can magnify change in society. *The Giant*, a work in the Scale Relationship Series by Cindy Sherman, is held in the Guggenheim Museum collection. [**Fig. 11**] Sherman created this 1967 collage from a series of photographs of herself as Paul Bunyan, wearing a Western lumberjack outfit: rolled-up denim jeans, flannel work shirt, longshoreman's hat with tall work boots. This was a subtler form of protest through work wear: abstracting stereotypically masculine Western clothing items and softening gender boundaries through design. Overt dissent like the Flint

Fig.11
The Giant, from the Scale Relationship
Series by Cindy Sherman, 1976

POWER TO THE PEOPLE: EVERYDAY DRESS AS PROTEST

Fig.12 (opposite)
Nelson Mandela by Robert
McCurdy, 2009

Fig.13 (right)
Headscarf worn by a member of
Las Madres de la Plaza de Mayo,
December 21, 2011

picket lines are straightforward and immediate; covert protests, instead, move slowly, seeping into the cultural consciousness. Sherman made her Paul Bunyan collage in the late 1960s, yet gay marriage has only become legal in the United States within the past ten years.

Throughout the twentieth century, the Western clothes explored above have become globalized. Folk dress, traditional clothing, and tribal dress have, across the world, been replaced by jeans, T-shirts, tennis shoes, and baseball caps. But fascinating shifts happen when traditional dress is used as a signal of social change. South African anti-apartheid leader Nelson Mandela fused colorful African wax cloth with the collared, tailored Western dress shirt to fashion his own symbol of freedom. As a young politician, Mandela frequently wore Western suits and ties. During some of his trials from 1961 to 1963 (he was accused of sabotage, violent uprising, and treason) he wore the tribal dress of his Xhosa clan, the kaross. Once he was able to cast off his prison uniform upon release in 1990, he transformed his wardrobe to match his politics by inventing a new form of folk dress. The Madiba shirt (Madiba was his Xhosa clan name) was Mandela's sartorial activism. As president of South Africa, he would be endlessly photographed next to world leaders in the casual, short-sleeved, wildly patterned shirts, worn untucked. [Fig.12]

The printed, colorful textile Mandela wore from the 1990s until his death in 2013 had deep roots in eighteenth- and nineteenth-century colonial trade. The wax cloth, printed with wood blocks in a rainbow of colors, was developed by Dutch textile designers and exported to Africa. Yinka Shonibare, the Nigerian artist who uses wax cloth in his elegant installations notes that "African fabric signifies African identity…rather like American jeans, [Levi's] are an indicator of trendy youth culture."[4] Shonibare explains that reclaiming the colonial symbol of wax cloth and recasting it as one of African pride "becomes an aesthetics of defiance, an aesthetics of reassurance, a way of holding on to one's identity in a culture presumed foreign or different."[5]

Headscarves (along with bandanas, kerchiefs, and handker-chiefs) have also crossed over from traditional dress for use as a tool for dissent. During the 1970s, an Argentinian military dicta-torship persecuted, kidnapped, and often killed the young adult children of a group of women, now grandmothers, who came to be called Las Madres de la Plaza de Mayo (the Mothers of the Plaza de Mayo). The desaparecidos (or disappeared) children were ini-tially kidnapped for alleged crimes against the nation, and many are thought to be dead. The women have been marching weekly in the Plaza de Mayo since 1977 and still do, wearing handmade white headscarves and demanding justice for the "disappeared," their children, whose names are commemorated in delicate blue cross-stitching on the cotton kerchiefs. [Fig.13] Now in their eighties and nineties, the mothers and grandmothers may not live to see justice, but they will leave a lasting symbol of folk liberty.

Made by hand from two or three deerskins and painted with stars, moons, birds, and suns, Ghost Dance garments, precious relics of Native American Ghost Dances, are housed in a few muse-ums across the United States and Canada. [Fig.14] In the late 1900s, a spiritual leader named Wovoka energized the Nevada Paiute tribe with the promise that Ghost Dances, done in secret around a bonfire at night, would banish white settlers and reclaim the land. News of the Ghost Dances traveled by word of mouth to neighbor-ing tribes, and many joined the movement. Massacres of Native people were already underway in the Southwest, with many tribes

Fig.14
Ghost Dance shirt, Museum of Native
American Heritage, ca. 1890–1900.
Photograph by Matt Rowe

forced to abandon their traditional dress, cut their hair, and wear
Western hand-me-downs. Ghost Dancers would create their regalia
from scratch; each garment was unique, customized with the mak-
er's hopes and dreams, and hidden away at daybreak. We all know
how the story ends: the Ghost Dances didn't stop the massacres,
even as tribes, like the Lakota, used the spiritual practice as a form
of resistance.

When drought hit the farmers of Tamil Nadu, India, in 2016
and the Indian government offered almost no aid, the village men
took extreme measures to capture national attention. Wearing the
traditional dress of Indian women, the sari, the men cross-dressed,
held live mice in their mouths, and shaved half their heads to agitate for change. [Fig.15] The month-long action worked: the Indian
government funded loans to sustain the farmers, and the saris
were returned to their wives. In a community where traditional

DRESSING THE RESISTANCE

Fig. 15 (opposite)
Tamil Nadu drought protesters,
New Delhi, India, April 14, 2017

Fig. 16 (right)
Paul Revere by John Singleton
Copley, 1768

dress and gender roles are typically set in stone, a simple change in how clothing is worn can give voice to the oppressed.

Saris serve as everyday dress but also function as a living record of the sophisticated cloth heritage of the Indian subcontinent. As John Gillow notes in his book *Traditional Indian Textiles*: "The interaction of peoples—invaders, indigenous tribes, traders and explorers—has built a complex culture legendary for its vitality and color; today, over ten million weavers, dyers, embroiderers and spinners contribute their handmade textiles to this melting pot."[6]

Handmade, humble textiles are woven into the history of another melting pot as well. The American Revolution was visually reflected in eighteenth-century oil paintings that depict rebels fighting against the English crown. Founders like Paul Revere, George Washington, John Adams, and Thomas Hutchinson rejected

I Sell the Shadow to Support the Substance.
SOJOURNER TRUTH.

English and French imports and instead whipped up patriotic zeal for homespun dress, often woven and sewn by their wives, servants, or slaves.

A 1768 portrait by American painter John Singleton Copley shows Paul Revere in a simple period shirt with soft collar, woven from natural fibers. [Fig.16] He wears an unembellished dark blue woolen waistcoat, which he would have paired with a matching set of plain breeches and leather shoes made by a local cobbler. In essence, these were propaganda portraits, not casual paintings. According to David C. Ward and Dorothy Moss, the fact that "Paul Revere was first a silversmith was essential to his activism as a revolutionary; the republican ideology of American radicalism was rooted in the skills and crafts of artisans."[7]

Similarly, in caricatures and etchings of the time, President Thomas Jefferson was shown wearing ragtag period shirts billowing out of a pair of breeches. King George of England was usually depicted wearing a fine silk three-piece suit, while French Emperor Napoléon Bonaparte was caricatured in overblown ceremonial military dress. The clothing says it all: Jefferson's simple, pared-down Protestant look clashes with the gold braid, rare feathers, expensive woven silks, and precious metals that the European rulers had imported from their colonies. Nationalists wanted to

Fig.17 (left)
Free Labor dress, Rokeby Museum, ca. 1850s

Fig.18 (right)
Sojourner Truth, carte de visite, 1864

cease trade with Europe, yearning for self-sufficiency, and home-spun goods were essentially the marketing and branding tools that revolutionaries used to spin their message.

The free produce movement took homegrown dress a step further. Hoping to pressure slave owners to consider abolition, free produce activists boycotted home goods, textiles, and supplies made with slave labor. A dark brown 1850s women's gown worn by Vermont housewife Rachel Robinson was spun from cotton, silk, and wool and was created freely and sustainably. [Fig.17] While keeping the style lines of the time—fitted bodice, long and narrow sleeves, full skirt, petticoat—it was pared down and devoid of the typical patterns, colors, and embellishments. If it looks strangely familiar, it's probably because the shape is reminiscent of gowns worn in *The Handmaid's Tale*, an ironic commentary on how long the need for suffrage has lasted.

From her name to her clothing, Sojourner Truth remade herself into a walking, talking icon of the abolitionist movement. A born-again, devout Methodist, she took the name Sojourner Truth (her original name, Isabella Baumfree, was given to her when she was born in 1797 into slavery in New York). After extreme hardships, she was freed. When setting out on lecture tours across the United States, Truth would wear a version of the free produce dress: modest, plain cloth with a white kerchief covering her hair. Pictured in this attire in a "carte de visite" (a vintage selfie, or an early Facebook profile photo), this was one of the few ways activists like Truth could connect with people who could not read. [Fig.18] Knowing that this might be the only picture that people would see of her during their lifetimes, Truth used her personal image and dress to further the abolitionist cause.

Over one hundred years later, as tanks burned in the background, a CIA photographer captured two young men in workaday trousers, jackets, and leather boots, waving a Czechoslovak flag as a new revolution erupted. [Fig.19] The Soviet invasion of 1968 pitted fellow Eastern European citizens against each other, as Czech civilians begged Russian soldiers to turn around and head back home in the early days of the occupation. While many photographers captured the scene as communist tanks rolled through one of Prague's most famous thoroughfares, Vaclavske Namesti, soon-to-be-famous Magnum photographer Joseph Koudelka perched himself high above the square, capturing iconic moments of the civil unrest in his own country. While each item Koudelka photographed was a legacy of working-class dress (the jeans, short

Fig.19
Czech Revolution protesters, Prague,
Czechoslovakia, 1968

utilitarian jackets, collared work shirts and boots), the clothes began to harmonize into a visual 1960s counterculture style. Spurred into activism by the invasion, young Czechs scribbled protest slogans on their jeans with pens and markers, and elevated ordinary dress into a visual messaging tool.

The next chapter explores how everyday dress becomes counterculture style when humankind pairs art, music, cinema, and dance with the act of rebellion. Ordinary clothes, remixed by younger generations exploring new ideas, become the defining imagery of an era: take the Beatles, add the latest 1960s liberal values and working-class teens desperate for a creative outlet, and you have a style zeitgeist. If culture is a way for society to encode its history and legacy, then counterculture seeks to dismantle those values in creating new social orders. Culture is our way of taking what's important to society and neatly packaging it into a set of principles that we can use almost as a manual, a guide to who we are. Anarchists, agitators, and activists have deployed counterculture trends to express overt and covert dissent from governments and rulers, restrictions on personal freedom, and outdated notions of gender roles, class restrictions, and racial equity.

CHAPTER 2

Shock the System: Subculture and Street Style

"I don't say we all ought to misbehave. But we ought to look as if we could."

—*Oscar Wilde*

Take an everyday garment—if you change its meaning to society, you can reshape it from a regular piece of clothing into a cipher. Punks across the world transformed a simple safety pin into a symbol of 1970s angst, anger, and anarchy. Young urban men in the 1950s turned a traditional men's dress suit into an outrageous postwar protest symbol by simply changing the cut, shape, and amount of fabric used. These changes can be subtle or loud—either way, society notices them and reacts. Youth street style of the 1950s was a perfect form of rebellion. Even poorer kids could get a hold of a few bits of fashion, join a group or gang, and walk the streets of any city in the Western world, shocking passersby as they went. Middle-class teenagers, with more disposable income, could rebel from the safety of their suburban neighborhoods, copying fashion trends.

In the previous chapter, we saw how everyday dress helps frame culture, society, and history, and reflects them back at us. But what happens when rebels take it a step further, actively disrupting? Some subcultures and countercultures take the building blocks of mainstream society, smash them, and reform the debris into new ways of thinking. Eric R. Wolf, writing about "cultural sets" (or trends in culture) in *Europe and the People Without History* (1982), shows that "in the course of action, these cultural sets are forever assembled, dismantled and reassembled, conveying in variable accents the divergent paths of groups and classes."[1]

Design historian Dick Hebdige and psychologist Rollo May both delved deeply into twentieth-century subcultures, like those of punks, mods, rockers, and new wavers, unpacking the philosophy behind rebellion and rules. They discovered that many subculture movements are similar in ideology, though purposefully different in dress. Clothing is a crucial expression of how the human race sanctions resistance and leaves space for rebellion. Recent emo, goth, rockabilly, and "brony" (men who adore the children's show *My Little Pony*) subcultures are made possible by "mainstream" society; subcultures disobey the regimented rules and morals that society internally creates.

It is precisely because society allows space for disobedience that counterculture and protest can exist and flourish. In examining peasant rebellions, author James C. Scott notes that "the parameters of resistance are also set, in part, by the institutions of repression."[2] In essence, a democratic government provides the fuel for the rebellion, protecting free speech, even if it is against the state. Only a totalitarian state can crush all forms of subculture:

if any and all rebellion ends in death, then the stakes are often too high for resistance to evolve.

In 1930s Maoist China, families wore a strict uniform of the utilitarian Mao suit to display their allegiance to and unity with the state and against capitalism and individuality. Mao Zedong and his third wife, He Zizhen, wore the same uniform as their people, emphasizing conformity within a regime so tight that a subculture of any kind would have been impossible. The risk of walking the street as a punk might have meant imprisonment or death, not only for oneself but also for one's family. Safety was an everyday concern, and the Mao suit was essentially protection from persecution. There must be a certain amount of freedom in a culture to make room for rebellion.

In Columbia Pictures' 1953 black-and-white flick *The Wild One*, Marlon Brando became an instant pop-culture figure as outlaw biker Johnny Strabler. [Fig.1] His costume reflected an authentic 1950s working-class rebel movement that started with postwar youth biker clubs and culminated in one of the most iconic and long-lasting menswear and womenswear looks of the twentieth and early twenty-first centuries: leather motorcycle jacket, T-shirt, jeans, and boots. In his 1994 autobiography, *Brando: Songs My Mother Taught Me*, he notes, "I was as surprised as anyone when T-shirts, jeans and leather jackets suddenly became symbols of rebellion."[3] Fueled by American cult idols like Brando and James Dean, utilitarian dress became fashion overnight, dragging the original act of teen protest into the spotlight with it.

Music, cinema, and clothing chased each other in an endless loop throughout the second half of the twentieth century. Enthusiastically consumed by the middle classes as they enjoyed their postwar leisure time and immortalized in the musical *West Side Story* (1957) and movies like *Grease* (1978) and *The Outsiders* (1983), youth resistance movements gave a budding generation of teenagers something to cling onto after the trauma and devastation of World War II. A new music form, rock, sparked a fashion trend, which in turn ignited dance styles that were reflected back at eager audiences in contemporary films and on stage. New media, photography, album covers, and modern art gave counterculture movements additional tools for provocation and created a modern way to deliver ideas to the masses.

Hoping to intimidate anyone who saw them on the street, white working-class teddy boys in 1950s suburban England crafted a retro look evoking aristocratic Edwardian tailoring. [Fig.2] "Teds"

Fig.1 (opposite)
Marlon Brando, film still from
The Wild One, 1953

wore three-piece fitted suits with velvet lapels, thick-soled "creeper" shoes and exaggerated ducktail hairstyles. Jazz musician and critic George Melly wrote his firsthand account (*Revolt into Style*, 1970) about the birth of pop culture, and describes how the teddy boys used their clothes: "The Teddy Boy and his successors were, in their way, artists. Their bodies were their canvas."[4] Part performance artists, part violent street gang dandies, the teddy boys ("teddy" coming from a nickname for King Edward VII of England) subverted an upper-class style to embody their lower-class anarchy. As fresh ideas bounced back and forth between England and the United States, dress styles strengthened ties between disenfranchised subcultures. Across the Atlantic, the teddy boys had a counterpart in postwar America: the zoot suiters.

Young Latinx soldiers returned home to a post–World War II American society that treated them as second-class citizens, simply based on the color of their skin. Angry, marginalized, and unrecognized for their military sacrifices, they proudly took up space on urban streets in fabric-wasting "zoot suits" to rebel against racism and inequity. The zoot suit was a fashion backlash against the plain, frugal, off-the-rack, rationed men's suits of the war. Early on in

Fig.2

Teddy boys, Sheffield, England, 1950s

Fig.3 (left)
World War II–era zoot suit, 1943

Fig.4 (right)
Zoot Suit Riot victims, Los Angeles,
June 7, 1943

the trend, bootleg tailors sprang up in 1930s New York City to fill bespoke orders from flamboyant customers, who, swathed in yards of expensive wool fabric, would go out in the evening to dance and socialize. In his autobiography, Black Power movement leader Malcolm X recollects buying his first zoot suit in 1940, joining the New York jazz counterculture movement in Harlem.[5] The trend blazed across America, and as the war progressed and fabric rationing became the norm, zoot suits were seen as unpatriotic, wasteful, and rebellious.

In 1943, police turned a blind eye to sailors disembarking their battleships in the ports around Los Angeles, looking for zoot suiters to punish. The lone zoot suiter above poses in a knee-length jacket and voluminous ultra-high-waisted trousers, complete with a white shirt, tie, lace-up leather shoes, and a pompadour hairstyle. [**Fig.3**] Outside of a cinema on June 7, 1943, at the height of the Los Angeles Zoot Suit Riots, Latinx and Black men faced danger when they stepped out on the street: zoot suits were ripped from their bodies by servicemen, policemen, and white passersby as punishment for wearing such overtly offensive fashion. [**Fig.4**] Arrests of the zoot suit victims, but not the sailors, followed. Journalist

Fig.5

Rude Boys, *Life* magazine photo essay,
Watts Towers, Los Angeles, July 1966

Stuart Cosgrove writes that the zoot suiters were "a spectacular reminder that the social order had failed to contain their energy and difference."[6] These rebels were the famous face of a wider Chicano/Latinx culture: pachucos, and their female counterparts, pachucas, listened to jazz and swing music, and developed "caló," a coded dialect for secret communication, akin to Jamaican patois—another coded dialect heard in reggae music.

Pachucas created their own version of a zoot suit, framing their pompadour hairstyles and dark eyeliner with prominent shoulder pads. They replaced the baggy trousers with knee-length pencil skirts and added heels, and dressing up became their form of resistance. Traditions of Latinx activism through music and clothes continued in the Chicano pride movements of the 1970s, the vibrant 1980s and 1990s cholo and chola culture, and reached into contemporary rap and hip-hop music and fashion.

In 1960s Jamaica, street culture burst onto the scene. Rudeboys, young men discontented with dim job prospects, racism, and rampant unemployment, rebelled by donning clothes inspired by American jazz musicians of the era: fitted ankle-length trousers, neat short-sleeved shirts with tidy collars, and small-brimmed straw hats. Electrified by the jazz music scene, the rudeboy look ricocheted from Jamaica to the United States, spreading from East to West Coast. A 1966 photograph from *Life* magazine documents the youth culture and street gangs of Watts, in South Los Angeles. [**Fig.5**] Each young man puts their own individual twist on the look (a generous flash of red sock, a camel shawl-collared cardigan) but simultaneously keeps in strict harmony with the overall look.

This style echoed across American youth culture as well—in fact, you can still see a strong rudeboy influence in contemporary everyday wear—think Bruno Mars with his neat suits, sunglasses, and cropped pants. Dress historian Valerie Steele in her 1985 book, *Fashion and Eroticism*, explores how fashion precedes social change rather than following it. Almost like a weather vane, changes in taste, style, and trends can warn of turbulent transition in culture and society. The rudeboys were the warning signs of post–World War II culture shifts like a Caribbean diaspora emigrating to Europe and the United States, the rise of teenage pop culture, and a growing desire for civil rights.

Once Jamaican rudeboy style hit England through immigrants from the Caribbean, local subcultures were electrified by the slick fashions. Mod style borrowed silhouettes from rudeboy dress and absorbed Black music like jazz, ska, and reggae. Photographer Janette Beckman captured the mod charm and sharp manner of the Islington twins in black and white. [**Fig.6**] Eye-catching in their identical outfits, school-aged twins Chet and Joe Okonkwo set up camp at the Highbury tube station in North London. The first mod wave in the 1960s was primarily white and working class, and like the teddy boys, mods ignited gang fights with rivals. The 1979 movie *Quadrophenia* was a raucous documentation of rumbles near English seaside towns, between rockers on motorcycles and mods on decked-out scooters. The Islington twins were part of an ultracool revival wave of mod culture in the 1970s and 1980s, and the brothers still dress in similar dapper looks to this day.

Twentieth-century menswear trends in the Western world were often influenced by Black culture. During the Harlem Renaissance, jazz began as protest music, and the clothes that followed flourished as protest clothes. As jazz and reggae sounds influenced mod and rudeboy fashion, musicians created a separate cultural identity firmly rooted in Black creativity. Legendary Black tenor saxophonist Sonny Rollins paid homage to Native American struggles for equality by wearing an early form of the Mohawk in

48

the late 1950s, inspired by a Mohawk tribal member he met at gigs. Because of him, the Mohawk became a rebel symbol years before punk made it iconic.

In the 1970s, more aggressively radical subcultures exploded into the void left by teddy boys, rockers, pachucos, and mods as most grew up, had families, and settled down to a more conventional lifestyle. Rumor has it that aging teddy boys scuffled with the fledgling punks on London's streets as the torch was passed from one subculture to another. Anarchic bands like the Clash absorbed contemporary social norms then shredded, destroyed, and re-formed them into new rules and aesthetics. But without those original social norms of post–World War II England, the Clash and their followers would have had nothing to destroy. Take reggae, the soul sound of West Indian music. Punk musicians abstracted reggae, ska, and dubstep into noise, tearing it from its Black West Indian roots but giving it a new life for a new uprising.

Fig.8
Harajuku fashion, Tokyo, January 8,
2018

London-based Vivienne Westwood, the illustrious first lady of
punk style, was a master of what Dick Hebdige calls "confronta-
tional dressing." Westwood started by cutting, shredding, printing,
dyeing, and knitting clothes for rebels, artists, and musicians in
her Chelsea shop (first called SEX, later World's End). In a color
photograph of her at SEX, she wears a classic white shirt (but
subverts it with the text "Be Reasonable, Demand the Impossible")
and is joined by shop assistant Jordan, writer Alan Jones, musician Chrissie Hynde, and Steve Jones of the Sex Pistols. [Fig.7] Their
bondage gear, latex, exposed breasts, unzipped pants, spiked hair,
and ghoulish makeup invited hatred and revulsion from 1970s
mainstream society. Punks gleefully took this rejection and fueled
the movement with it. The more revolting they were, the stronger
their message of anarchy became.

Westwood herself stated that she was done with the punk
movement in the 1980s, when it was no longer shocking. Always
searching for the next form of expression, Westwood transformed
herself into a lifelong student of historical dress, delving into
the rich archives at the National Art Library, tucked away on the

second floor of the Victoria and Albert Museum in London, and immersing herself in pattern books like Nora Waugh's *The Cut of Men's Clothes*.[7] Mixing precise historical research with cutting-edge high-end fashion sparked an alchemy that has made Westwood a global influencer and rebel to this day—her dresses are worn by celebrities around the globe, and at seventy-nine, wearing her own designs, she still joins street protests for climate change and social justice.

A crucial legacy of the punk movement was the use of common objects as visual symbols of rebellion. From household object to punk accessory, the safety pin is revisited again by a Harajuku trendsetter. [Fig.8] He wears a sequined jacket over denim, hundreds of safety pins glittering as they hang off chain necklaces, and a bronze skull mask encrusted with even more pins, earrings, trinkets, and chains. At first, this style may not appear to be protest or activism, but it began as a gentle form of dissent by young Japanese women who craved alternate forms of female beauty. After exposure through street-style photography, social media, and fashion blogs, Harajuku is now famous as a joyous form of personal expression.

By the 1980s, subcultures themselves had fragmented into a myriad of micromovements, each with their own set of complex rules. One of the most recognizable was the skinhead movement, born of punk but tilting toward white nationalism and violence toward immigrants rather than anarchy and atheism aimed at the establishment. Skinheads pared down the punk look, eventually losing the Mohawk and makeup but keeping the heavy boots and denim jeans, mashing them up with the mod and rudeboy influences of neat polo shirts, suspenders, and shaved heads. While current alt-right skinheads agitate for racial separation, they ironically celebrate the rich legacy of Black counterculture style of the mods and rudeboys with their clothes. In a photo taken by Terence Spencer in 1969, skinheads stalk past a gathering of hippies on the steps of Piccadilly Circus in London, their clothing showing how polarized the subcultures had become. [Fig.9]

An iconic photograph by Bernie Boston shows an anonymous young hippie placing a single flower into the barrel of a National Guardsman's rifle. [Fig.10] While the identity of this young man remains a mystery, legend has it that he drove from New York to the National Mall protest in 1967 with poet and activist Allen Ginsberg, who encouraged the use of flowers and music as a positive form of counterculture expression.[8] This was a softer form of

Fig.9 (opposite top)
Skinheads, Piccadilly Circus, London, New Years Day, 1969

Fig.10 (opposite bottom)
Anti–Vietnam War protests, Washington, DC, April 8, 1967

Fig.11 (top)
Gustav Klimt outside his artist's studio in Vienna, Austria, 1912

Fig.12 (bottom)
"American Fashions," The Jno. J. Mitchell Litho. Co., New York, August 1899

counterculture: a comfortable turtleneck sweater and tousled sun-bleached hair, devoid of violence and angst. The hippie subculture, with its flower children and peaceniks, took its inspiration from earlier movements, like the Pre-Raphaelites, aesthetes, and the original Bohemians.

In his studio, wearing only a long linen smock and simple leather sandals (and apparently, no undergarments), Austrian artist Gustav Klimt painted erotic, dreamy works, often shocking the European art establishment. [**Fig.11**] Throughout the last half of the nineteenth century, the average middle-class Western man would have worn a fitted three-piece suit, tailored shirt with a stiff starched collar, a tie, and lace-up leather boots, accessorized with a hat, cane, and pocket watch, as shown in this 1899 menswear catalog lithograph. [**Fig.12**] And that was just for daytime. Strict rules also governed how men should dress in the evening, while hunting or playing a sport, and for traveling. The rigid, prescriptive social rules around menswear in the nineteenth century gave reformers and artists (as we'll see in the following images) something to resist against and some rules to break. Klimt's liberated choice of modest smock, which would still draw curious glances in the Western world today, would have branded him as a Bohemian in his time.

Rejecting the structured, regimented lifestyle of the Industrial Revolution, Bohemians (named after Bohemia, a western region of Czech Republic and the location of Prague, the epicenter of European counterculture) disrupted late-nineteenth-century society with innovations in design, dress, and lifestyle. Unisex clothing (like Klimt's smock, and similar versions worn by women at that time) is often a sign that change is coming: it's a response to a society that desires to divide binary genders into strict social roles. The Bohemian movement disdained established rules and set the stage for disruptive social change.

Elite dress reformers like Gustav Klimt moved in the same circles as dandies like writer Oscar Wilde and Bohemians like actress Sarah Bernhardt, living in and traveling between European capitals like London, Paris, Prague, and Berlin. With literary salons, operas, theaters, and private dinners to attend they needed beautiful clothes that visually reflected their ultramodern ideals. The following photograph of a piece by Mariano Fortuny, a Spanish-born painter-turned-designer, from the Victoria and Albert Costume and Textile Collection documents a diaphanous whisper of a dress, made of black silk that would pool at the feet of the wearer. [**Fig.13**] The simplicity of the gown depended on hidden drawstrings and

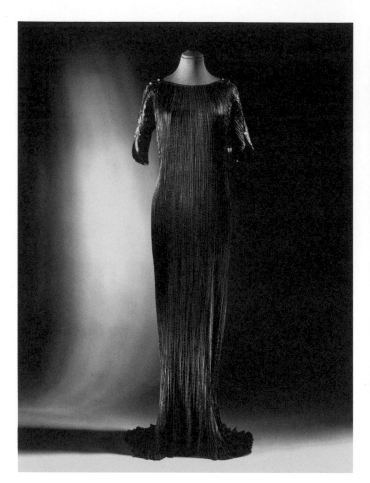

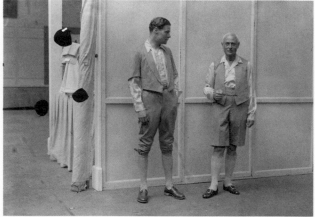

thin lacing tipped with delicate Venetian glass beads. Fortuny worked from his palace in Venice, creating theatrical lighting and sets before turning his hand to textiles and gowns based on classical Greek principles of design. Compared to the structured, tightly corseted, and synthetically dyed dresses of the Victorian era, Fortuny's gowns were truly revolutionary. An artist or socialite would have worn this gown to symbolize a new, harmonious ideal that drew inspiration from the natural world.

The men's dress reform movement in the early twentieth century further dismantled dress codes and social expectations obsessed with health and bodily liberation. Doctor Gustav Jaeger's Sanitary Woollen System, worn by explorers and newly minted sports fanatics, urged the public to wear hygienic woolen long johns instead of regular underwear. Not only clothes but lifestyle signaled this change: the invention of health food came soon after, and dress reformers urged followers to exercise and take the air. In June of 1930, the Men's Dress Reform Party advocated for a new form of evening dress. In a 1930 photograph, two party members model the inventive new look: shorts with suits, capelet jackets, knee-length socks, and a renegade approach to neckwear. [**Fig.14**]

Fig.13 (left)
Delphos evening dress, Mariano Fortuny, 1920

Fig.14 (top right)
Men's Dress Reform Party members, June 23, 1930

Fig.15 (bottom right)
Oscar Wilde, photograph by Napoleon Sarony, 1882

54

Writer Oscar Wilde, who may look old fashioned to our modern eye, was an exemplar dandy of his day—in 1880s London, he would have been the most thrilling, scandalous dresser at any dinner party, opera, or salon. While English royalty and the aristocratic establishment would have been wearing the restrictive, tailored dress described above, Wilde boldly and meticulously concocted an avant-garde image. [Fig.15] Instead of fitted trousers, he wore eighteenth-century-style knee breeches (knickerbockers); instead of tailored suit jackets, soft velvet smoking jackets; and silk stockings with delicate patent-leather pumps. This was a man who was not working in a factory, needing practical, durable clothes, but following the aesthetic ethos "art for art's sake." Wilde became a work of art himself, encoding ciphers in his clothes by wearing a rich dark green color that symbolized homosexuality, dressing in folk costumes, and cultivating a relaxed elegance that rebelled against society's carefully constructed Victorian dress codes.

In her 1968 article on the aesthetic movement, Leonee Ormond underlines how this romantic, idealistic movement used dress for social change: "With a subtle combination of exhibitionism and reforming fervor, the aesthetes went out of their way to be conspicuous. In their appearance, they tried to reverse the sex-roles. While the men carried large flowers or wore effeminate velveteen knickerbockers, the women showed their scorn for contemporary fashion by deliberately designing unfeminine clothes."[9] Blurring gender lines, which were entrenched in Victorian lifestyle and dress, was a way for Wilde and his circle to rebel.

Meanwhile, Russian nihilists conjured a dark, gloomy version of reform dress as they set out to erase all meaning from the world. Swiping away ideas of romanticism, idealism, and aestheticism, nihilists lived only for today: they were the early atheist punks of 1870s Russia. Daily life in the Czarist regime was punishing, and nihilists (from the Latin *nihil*, meaning "nothing") were political radicals, forming underground societies and revolutionary training programs, hoping to overthrow the oppressive government.

Calling themselves the "new people," nihilist men borrowed from European peasant dress and work wear, fashioning a monochromatic, minimalist visual identity, complete with a homespun cloak for warmth. "To signal their emancipation, they abandoned the elegant manners and costumes of their parents in favour of greater simplicity," wrote historian and author Christine Ruane in *Fashioning the Body Politic*.[10] Like Wilde and the dress reformers, nihilists abandoned traditional nineteenth-century gender roles, believing that women should be equal to men and reflecting these ideals with simple woolen dresses and cropped hair. In 1881, artist and military general Nikolai Yaroshenko painted a lone student against a stark pastoral background, embodying new hope for the people through equitable and austere dress. [Fig.16]

Subcultures are still alive and well in our globally connected world, and we can use them to see what's important to us right now. A simple hat can be the object of our case study. Although a century apart, English painter Augustus John and American musician Pharrell Williams have rocked the same headwear. [Figs.17, 18] This may not seem significant, until we see that history and design can be our guides to differentiating between one-off moments and major cultural shifts. John was a turn-of-the-nineteenth-century rebel in handcrafted shirts and peasant-style sandals that reflected a growing trend toward a return to nature and a yearning for a simpler lifestyle after the automation of the Industrial Revolution. Williams is a turn-of-the-twentieth-century rebel, a cutting-edge, award-winning musician who uses his fame and fashion to reframe Black male identity and masculinity, wearing shorts with tuxedo jackets to red-carpet events, just like the members of Men's Dress Reform Party did eighty years earlier.

What these two men have in common, besides a hat, is that they embody larger societal changes. The image of John in simple clothes, crouched in an empty courtyard, encapsulates the technology fatigue many people were feeling at the end of the nineteenth century, echoed in the handmade Fortuny dresses and Klimt's linen artist smock. One hundred years later, humankind has left the twentieth century behind, with new technology introduced for a new millennium. Only a few decades into the twenty-first century, much of humankind is already overconnected by computers, phones, and Wi-Fi. Feeling a similar fatigue to a different technological advance, the current hipster subculture embraces many of the same visual cues as the Victorian aesthetes: a love of heritage brands like Levi's, who recently reintroduced an exact copy of their first 501® original denim jean from the 1890s, handwoven natural-fiber textiles from brands like New York–based Ace & Jig, and handmade leather footwear from the aptly named Ancient Greek Sandals brand.

Simultaneously dipping into the heritage aesthetic while creating his own, Williams launched the Billionaire Boys Club clothing line, a rap- and hip-hop-inspired brand of street wear, with an eclectic mix of color choices, sportswear style, unisex pieces,

Fig.16
The Student by Nikolai Alexandrovich Yaroshenko, 1881

Fig.17 (left)
Augustus John by Charles F. Slade, 1909

Fig.18 (right)
Pharrell Williams, Los Angeles, March 29, 2014

and even rhinestones. Billionaire Boys Club joins other hip-hop brands, like RocaWear, Phat Farm, Wu Wear, and Yeezy, in creating a cultural explosion of Black street-wear design. Williams's status as a style icon inspires haute-couture designers to collaborate with him—the tall, felted fedora (with the crown knocked out) that Williams wears is from Vivienne Westwood's recent collection, bringing punk and subculture full circle. The hat went viral, and mass fashion knocked off the look, which was eagerly worn by fans across the world. Gender equality and freedom has, along with technology, become a defining characteristic of the twenty-first century, and Williams rolls all this into his personal identity.

The artists, actors, musicians, writers, and poets in this chapter all gravitated toward counterculture to express dissent, galvanizing the younger generations, who then magnified the message. Subcultures elevate ordinary clothes into style revolutions—trends sometimes continue long after the original protests have died down. What happens, though, when we add money and power to ordinary dress? Fashion. In the next chapter, political disruptions occur in elite royal circles, through haute couture and bespoke tailoring, against a backdrop of war and revolution.

CHAPTER 3

Strut Your Stuff: Fashion and Elite Resistance

"Fashion is at its best a tyrannically democratic force."

—Quentin Bell, art critic and historian, 1947

When the COVID-19 pandemic hit, face masks suddenly became a part of our daily lives and quickly became a visual expression of our inner selves. Face masks have become politicized, polarized, and emotionally charged, representing the full range of human response to an unexpected worldwide event. No longer just a humble piece of cloth, the face mask is also a symbol, a cipher, and a billboard. Surprisingly, there is a deep connection between the social theories behind a simple face covering and elite fashion; they function in exactly the same way. Both are profoundly connected with how we make social choices and negotiate with each other.

While today the business of fashion revolves around global designer names, brands, labels, and couture houses, its origins lie in elemental human interactions. When we meet people, we instinctively want to know where we stand. For safety and survival, early humans needed to know immediately if a new group of people were friend or foe, a help or hindrance, an ally or competitor. Nonverbal clues that conveyed difference (a never before seen color, a new type of headdress, a new way of metalworking, a new natural resource) were decisive in analyzing the "other." This is fashion—a way to offer information about ourselves through difference, innovation, and competition.

In some sense, fashion has always been with us, but like culture, it changes as we change. While ancient Roman dress was relatively static compared to the pace of fashion today, trends did exist—for example, fine woolen shawls imported from the East into Western Europe. Ancient Egyptians expressed their love of adornment and decoration in changing wig and jewelry fashions across three thousand years, while China and Japan have been experimenting with makeup for millennia as a way to convey social hierarchy and influence. While early dress historians theorized that fashion was primarily a European construct, a more global and inclusive reading of cultural history shows that fashion and craft existed across most human cultures, dating back to late Neolithic woven string skirts.

In Europe, fashion as a sartorial practice began to accelerate more than a thousand years ago, visually recording the pace of cultural change as European royal courts jostled with each other for power. Each country customized their fashion, architecture, fine art, and literature to broadcast differences, highlighting national pride and distinguishing cultural characteristics. From the early medieval period onwards inventors developed new technology for spinning, weaving, milling, dyeing, and embroidering, and an endless loop of innovation pushed fashion forward as countries competed with each other for dominance. After the Industrial Revolution, air, train, and boat travel meant that fashion traveled across the globe faster, and now social media means that when the couture house Gucci markets a pandemic mask it can be telegraphed across the globe in seconds and sold out it minutes.

This chapter explores fashion theory and how fashion makes itself different from everyday dress and clothing. Fashion is the ideal partner for rebellion, and face masks provide the perfect analogy for how fashion works. The pandemic has reignited interest in social contracts, code-switching, and group-behavior theories. A simple social contract—*wear a mask in public*—has forced us to decide whether or not we will break the contract or obey this new social order: go maskless; or adapt our masks for protest, with slogans like "Black Lives Matter" or "Make America Great Again"; or use humor and irony, broadcasting "If You Can Read This, You Are Too Close" across our faces; or wear a plain disposable mask with nothing on it.

No wonder, then, that most social philosophers, like John Locke, Thomas Hobbes, Georg Simmel, J. C. Flügel, and Jean-Jacques Rousseau, have written about fashion theory. Building on the work of these early philosophers is the work of John Searle, who developed the discipline of social ontology in the 1960s. Ontology looks at how we communicate with each other and create order in our world. As members of society, we collectively agree on what rules to live by, in every aspect of our existence. Searle examined how we make pacts with each other, our families, our government, the police, and the military, and called these pacts "social contracts." Chaos can ensue when we break those pacts.

Fashion history is littered with broken social contracts. The ability of fashion to visually disrupt these agreements and norms makes it an exceptional tool for rebels. Designers are addicted to rule-breaking—it's how they innovate, so for them the question becomes how to decide which rules to break. You have to be in the know to be able to read the clues, visual hashtags, codes, and messages. Fashion designers become our translators and guides in decoding our own cultures. They observe society, are ahead of the curve, and obsessively look for what's next on the horizon all the while simultaneously looking to history for inspiration.

No investigation of history and rebellion would be complete without looking at the French Revolution, a perfect case study in

dress and social change. The twelve years of revolution between 1792 and 1804 overflowed with brand new social contracts, which were broken and re-formed at dizzying speed, reflected through changes in dress, accessories, and visual language. Entire books have been written on this complex topic, notably Aileen Ribeiro's *Fashion and the French Revolution* (1988) and Kimberly Chrisman-Campbell's *Fashion Victims: Dress at the Court of Louis XVI and Marie-Antoinette* (2015), but for this chapter we'll take a quick tour of the highlights.

French monarch Louis XIV gave fashion a well-deserved compliment when he said, "Fashion is the mirror of history. It reflects social, economic, and political change, rather than mere whimsy."

Little did he know how ironic his words would be, when his great-great-great grandson Louis XVI was beheaded in 1793 in the early years of the revolution. Louis XVI's luxurious lifestyle and fashion were a catalyst for the uprising, and he himself was reflected in the mirror of history. Aristocracy around the world has always used dress to reinforce their position in society, and at the onset of the revolution, in 1792, King Louis XVI and Queen Marie Antoinette symbolized the excess and waste of the monarchy. In their portraits, we see the ciphers of the Ancien Régime: extravagant clothes, hair, accessories, jewelry, and furnishings. [Figs.2,3] The silk breeches worn by Louis XVI became the battleground for new fashions, as the elite refused to let go of their privilege as the eighteenth century waned.

As Christopher Breward mentions in his 1995 book *The Culture of Fashion*: "The aristocracy are generally seen as the initiators of elite innovation in fashionable dress. Certainly their activities and habits are those which are recorded most frequently."[1] Marie Antoinette, a notable example, was an outlier and an innovator. She connected political power and tastemaking in an intoxicating way, and her every move was documented. (It's a pity social media didn't already exist, because painting and portraiture were barely potent enough to record her luxurious lifestyle.)

It was this excess and luxury that ignited rebellion in the lower classes. Government regulations meant that the eighteenth-century French working class was perpetually poor, and theories of equality and democracy propelled them to revolt. Philosopher J. C. Flügel notes that "the new social order demanded something that expressed…the common humanity of all men…a uniformity achieved particularly by the abolition of those distinctions which had divided the wealthy from the poor, the exalted from the humble."[2] To that end, Louis XVI was renamed Citoyen (citizen) Louis Capet by the rebels, stripped of royal status, beheaded, and buried in an unmarked grave as an ordinary citizen.

The fashions that followed show how social contracts were made, broken, remade, and broken again. The revolution lasted ten years, with thousands executed during the Reign of Terror, and ended only when Napoléon Bonaparte staged a coup in 1799 and crowned himself emperor in 1804.

The rebels who imprisoned the king and his family styled themselves in the clothes of regular, working people. They were called the Third Estate, or the commoners, and followed strict social and sartorial rules. In a 1792 portrait by Louis-Léopold Boilly, an actor and singer named Chenard dresses as a sans culotte for a festival. He wears a short worker's jacket called the carmagnole, a striped waistcoat, the famous sans culottes (meaning "without breeches"), which were a kind of rugged woolen trousers, and wooden industrial clogs, usually worn in factories. [Fig.1] Every single item he wears on his body is an antifashion symbol. Even the wooden clogs have roots in rebellion. The word "sabotage" developed when clogs (called *sabots*) were thrown into machinery by factory workers disgruntled by poor working conditions during the Industrial Revolution.

The sans culottes were crucial in the executions of aristocrats during the Reign of Terror, and by wearing the clothing of the common man, they preserved their own lives. "During the Terror in particular, it was politically suspect to appear elegant; at best it implied a greater concern with one's appearance than with the benefit of people in general, and at worst it could be taken as almost a presumption of treason," writes Aileen Ribeiro, the dress historian, in her book *Fashion and the French Revolution*.[3] Ribeiro emphasizes how important it was to reject the vast luxury of Marie Antoinette and Louis XVI.

While the revolution raged around him, artist and rebel Jacques-Louis David tried to distill the political ideals of a nation into a single "civic costume." Inspired by the garb of ancient Greece and Rome, he sketched out variations of an egalitarian uniform that could be worn by all citizens and adapted to reflect rank, social status, and government duties. [Fig.4] It never made it to market. After many debates and discussions, the revolution had already moved on by the time the final civic costume was chosen, and it was left behind in the frenzied race of changing fashion.

Almost a postmodern commentary on the French Revolution, a late-eighteenth-century vest, or gilet, held in the dress archives at the Los Angeles County Museum of Art, is a marvel of ciphers, colors, and lettering. [Fig.5] The gilet is knitted with silk yarn and silk tufts, incorporating butterfly motifs and patriotic French phrases, such as *L'habit ne fait pas le moine*, or "the habit does not make the monk." Around the pale pink collar, the word *charmante*, or "charming," is stitched in neat cursive. Analyzing the wearer of this remarkable piece of history, author Kimberly Chrisman-Campbell writes, "Flaunting his revolutionary colors

Fig.5 (left)
Vest, France, 1789–94, Los Angeles County Museum of Art

Fig.6 (right)
Modes Parisienne, Merveilleuses et Incroyables, engraving after Carle Vernet, 1795

while protesting that clothes don't make the man, he wore his politics on his sleeve even as he distanced himself from them."[4] In a modern-day twist on this theme, adventure-gear company Patagonia wove overtly political messages into the tags of their Fall 2020 shorts line: "Vote those a—holes out."

In response to the sans culottes and militants, new tribes popped up all over Paris, carving out their own share of the revolution. The *muscadins*, named after a musk-scented perfume, were young working-class dandies with nothing to lose who prowled the streets at night with wooden clubs, looking for a fight. They wore exaggerated, expensive fashions, the tighter the better, and returned to wearing silk breeches in defiance of the sans culottes. In a macabre twist, the muscadins wore their collars and cravats ridiculously high, pretending to protect their necks from the guillotine, while their female counterparts, the *merveilleuses* (the marvelous ones), wore red ribbons around their necks to symbolize the blood of executions. The muscadins were also known as, and evolved into, the *incroyables* (the incredibles), who escorted

Fig.7 (above)
Josephine de Beauharnais, Empress of the French by François Gérard, 1801

Fig.8 (left)
Napoléon Bonaparte Premier Consul, Château de Chantilly by François Gérard, 1803

Fig.9 (opposite)
Wallis Simpson, Duchess of Windsor in the Elsa Schiaparelli "Lobster Dress," United Kingdom, 1937

the merveilleuses to balls and to the theaters and gardens of Paris. [Fig.6] As trends rapidly changed between 1794 and 1799, the styles of the upper classes were intermixed with lower-class looks, and the incroyables and merveilleuses seemed to have evolved to prize fashion over politics.

In the face of death all around them, the fashionable merveilleuses began dressing in sheer muslin gowns, cashmere shawls, feathers, silk ribbons, and light slippers rather than in the heavy cotton skirts, corsets, aprons, and woolen jackets made popular as the democratic working-class women's dress in the early days of the revolution. This was rebellion against the rebellion and another broken contract: while the merveilleuses dressed in a simple, neoclassical style, their clothes were still expensive, meticulous, and profoundly impractical. Long gone were the woolen trousers, dirty hair, and wooden clogs of the sans culottes, worn only a few years before. This glorious cornucopia of French Revolutionary clothing capped off the end of the eighteenth century, and waiting in the wings was Napoléon Bonaparte, ready to redirect the image of political fashion once again as the new millennium began.

A brand-new century would need a brand-new fashion system. As we've seen so far, fashion differs from everyday clothing—it thrives on fantasy, invention, and imagination rather than the reality of daily life. Napoléon would reach back to ancient Greece and Rome for visual inspiration. His empress, Joséphine, could not look more different than Marie Antoinette in an 1801 painting by François Gérard. [Fig.7] The empress, dressed in a whisper-thin cotton dress, sits on simple velvet cushions with a Greek column in the background, a neoclassical goddess in white. Similarly, in his portrait, Napoléon wears modest dress, inspired by military uniforms, and rejects the decoration of the Ancien Régime. [Fig.8] Both looks were radically different from the extravagantly crafted attire of the court of Louis XVI and Marie Antoinette, and Napoléon used ancient Greek styles to inspire the branding of his new democratic regime, not only dressing himself but his wife, household, government, and military with intentionally designed fashion, uniforms, furniture, and architecture.

Now, having explored the French Revolution and its encyclopedic use of fashion to riot and disrupt, let's turn to the twentieth century, where every decade was brimming with cultural change. Fashion seesaws right along with it as an endless array of new designers conjure up iconic looks for each new movement.

Fig.10
Odette Fabius, courtesy of Georgina Hayman, ca. 1942

The early twentieth century saw many antiestablishment art movements. After World War I and the concurrent Spanish flu, Europe, the United States, and the colonies had seen so much death and destruction that it was impossible to return to the old ways of life. Dadaism, surrealism, and anti-art movements all began to chip away at previous traditions, using surprising tools: a lobster as a telephone, a shoe in the shape of a hat, and found objects, like abandoned toilets, all became iconic design symbols. Avant-garde designer Elsa Schiaparelli created whimsical, subversive clothes, like black evening gloves with fingernails embroidered on the outside. The arts once again reflected immense social change at this time, fragmenting the ordered, realistic style of classical art into abstract and geometric works. And while the surrealists were dismantling art, Wallis Simpson, an American socialite, and the Prince of Wales were dismantling the rules of the English aristocracy, morality, and religion.

Simpson, twice divorced, was a consummate disrupter in the most stylish way possible, earning the nickname "royal rebel." Her husband-to-be, King Edward VIII of England, turned against the monarchy and old-fashioned notions of divorce, marriage, duty, and love by abdicating the English throne to marry Simpson. Their lavish lifestyle, luxury vacations, and sartorial style were closely watched, and in a photograph by Cecil Beaton, Simpson disrupted royal tradition by wearing a gown by Schiaparelli. [Fig.9] As a member of the surrealist art movement, fashion innovator Schiaparelli designed clothes that challenged the status quo. When Simpson wore the infamous 1937 "Lobster Dress" (based on Salvador Dali's paintings) when she sat for Beaton, she was reinforcing her determination to forge her own path rather than bow to the will of the monarchy. A champion of scandalous styles, she bucked tradition and wore a simple pale blue evening gown to her wedding. She was also an early adopter of Christian Dior's shocking New Look.

In a photo of World War II resistance member Odette Fabius, she wears couture by French designer Jeanne Lanvin that looks functional and utilitarian but, in fact, is made from expensive fabric and exquisite tailoring. [Fig.10] It would have taken weeks to make in a quiet atelier in Paris by *les petites mains*, or the "little hands," of haute couture—seamstresses, tailors, embroiderers, and hand-beading specialists. Georgina Hayman, Fabius's granddaughter, remembers that "whilst carrying precious allied secrets across France in her luggage, Odette Fabius was always proud, always elegant, always fearless. She had great charm and nerve with a razor sharp intellect that got her out of being arrested during the war many times. Her idea of going somewhere incognito was to not wear a hat and gloves!"[5]

Under Nazi control, women in 1940s occupied France deployed patriotic fashions to covertly demonstrate defiance. The Nazis forbade the French from wearing the expensive, hand-tailored haute couture beloved by the French elite in an effort to erode national pride. French women countered with haute couture that was so subtle in its fabric and technique that the Nazis couldn't recognize it. When the Nazis set up a department to review new hat designs and ban luxury fabrics, French women gathered discarded materials, such as crepe paper, straw, newspaper, and chicken feathers, to make extravagant (but free) millinery, finding a way to continue wearing French fashion even during a time of extreme restriction. [Fig.11] Covert signals were critical during this time, and women who could recognize the signs and codes could communicate through their fashions. When the war ended, the French couture industry survived the devastation and took innovation and craftsmanship to an even higher level.

French Philosopher Roland Barthes wrote extensively on how fashion can pivot rapidly to mirror social change. In his essays *Oeuvres Completes*, Barthes comments that: "Clothes live in close symbiosis with their historical context, much more than language. Violent historical episodes (wars, exoduses, revolutions) can rapidly smash a system: but in contrast to language, the re-casting of the system is much quicker."[6] In the case of Dior's 1947 New Look fashion zeitgeist, the "re-casting of the system" was so quick that protests broke out across major metropolitan cities. In Chicago, members of the "See Below the Knee Club" waited in front of Dior's hotel, chanting and holding signs that read "Mr. Dior: We Abhor Dresses to the Floor" as he exited. [Fig.12] Haute couture is an elite machine for experimentation and disruption, and after the strict textile rationing during World War II, Dior knew that using an abundance of fabric in his designs would be utterly shocking.

Morality and modernity were at stake when Dior suggested that women return to a tightly corseted, restrictive way of dressing, with hourglass-shaped jackets over full calf-length skirts. In contrast to the utilitarian, modest, and practical styles of World War II clothing, the New Look was glamorous and extravagant. Some women were thrilled at the hyperfeminine couture, while others rebelled against what they saw as a return to the old days. Wartime

Fig.11
Hat by fashion designer Rose Valois, FIDM Museum, 1942–44

Fig.12

Women picket fashion designer
Christian Dior in Chicago, Illinois, 1947

clothes were comfortable and meant for practicality, echoing the freedom women found when working outside the home as they replaced soldiers at war. Dior was suggesting women return to a time of being beautiful rather than useful. Luckily, one of Dior's contemporaries, designer Claire McCardell, showed women that they could have both with her fresh 1940s and 1950s styles, and for a time, both Dior's corseted New Look and McCardell's midriff-baring designs coexisted.

McCardell's impact is so profound that it still affects most clothing we wear today. But unlike Dior's New Look, which very publicly exploded onto the postwar scene, McCardell's superpower was that she created understated and subtle fashion while revolutionizing how women wore their garments. She created tailored, smart clothes that kept the feminine shape Dior had reimagined but did so without restriction. Firmly positioning her pieces for women who swam, vacationed, traveled, and worked, she carved out a space for practicality in a woman's wardrobe and implied through her designs that women should have as much mobility and opportunity as men, without sacrificing style. One 1944 ensemble, made from black linen with prominent white stitching, included a pair of play shorts and a cropped short-sleeve top. [**Fig.13**] The visible skin at the midriff gave the viewer a window to modernity: one could see for themselves that there was no old-fashioned corset, only a woman's natural shape.

Continuing the trend started by McCardell, millions of women welcomed the Youthquake movement looks of the 1960s. Modern hairstyles, miniskirts, and low heels all pointed toward a woman who was not trapped by her clothes but, instead, was liberated by them. Anyone who didn't get these social codes was left behind or found themselves outraged. One of the new fashion personalities, English designer Mary Quant lived the hip, ultramodern lifestyle she was selling. George Melly, author of *Revolt in Style*, notes that "Mary Quant came from an originally working-class Welsh background with parents who were earnest believers in the merits of plain living and high thinking, a very useful basis for the form her revolt took."[7] A photo of the designer in stark black and white shows her wearing her controversial miniskirt paired with a futuristic Vidal Sassoon haircut. [Fig.14] Quant and her equally stylish husband and business partner, English aristocrat Alexander Plunkett-Green, lived a thoroughly modern lifestyle and rebelled against morality codes and judgment from the Church of England and conservative social groups.

Another British fashion designer, Katharine Hamnett, started her career designing casual high-end pieces for the understatedly stylish and printing political messages on oversized 1980s T-shirts: "CHOOSE LIFE," "PROTECT AND SURVIVE," "STOP ACID RAIN." When she wore one of her own designs to meet Queen Elizabeth II, the entire country saw the bold black letters "58% DON'T WANT PERSHING" printed on her white tee (a reference to anti-nuclear missile activism across Europe), worn with white leggings and Converse. [Fig.15] The Queen was in a demure black velvet ensemble worn with an oversized silk pussy bow at the neck. The contrast was startling. In 2017, *Vogue* praised Hamnett as "London's Activist Fashion Warrior" after she became an advocate for ethical environmental practices in the fashion industry.[8]

When modern fashion is at its best, it is equitable, inclusive, and diverse. Italian brand Benetton started a wave of activism in the 1990s and early 2000s with provocative, socially progressive ad campaigns, which were selling fashion, of course, but via cultural disruption. Italian designer Gianni Versace broke the mold by using models of all genders and sexualities. A Helmut Red lipstick campaign, published in 2012 and photographed by Mark Seliger, features model Jenny Shimizu in the nude, accessorized only with a sharp pixie crop, tattoos, and the new red lip stain. Openly gay,

Fig.13
Ensemble by fashion designer
Claire McCardell, 1944

Shimizu was not tall, not white, and not conventionally beautiful, but her inclusion in the ad shows the power of fashion photography in opening our eyes to social change.

Jimmy Backius photographed a model in a hijab for *BON* magazine in 2002, starting an early trend of representing Muslim fashion in Western countries. And in 2019, Halima Aden broke barriers as *Sports Illustrated*'s first model in a hijab and burkini and became an advocate for diversity in fashion and beauty. [**Fig.16**] *Allure* magazine put her on their cover and declared her a "destroyer of stereotypes." She herself has said, "We all need representation."[9]

Equal representation is on the minds of a young African generation as well. Ten-year-old Okili currently lives in Brazzaville, Republic of Congo, and uses the unpaved dirt streets as his catwalk. He is a young sapeur. "Le Sape" is an abbreviation of Societe des Ambianceurs et des Personnes Elegantes (the Society of Tastemakers and Elegant People) and male sapeurs and female sapeuses dress in designer suits, accessories, and watches, although some don't even have running water or electricity. Why defy logic and spend money on luxurious fashion? *Al Jazeera* reporter Tariq Zaidi notes, "Over the decades, it has functioned as a form of colonial resistance, social activism and peaceful protest."[10] Sapeurs may wear regular clothes or work uniforms during

Fig.14 (left)
Fashion designer Mary Quant, 1967

Fig.15 (right)
Prime Minister Margaret Thatcher and Katharine Hamnett, Downing Street, London, 1984

76

Fig.16
Model Halima Aden, Los Angeles,
February 9, 2020

the day, but they morph into defiant tastemakers when dressing up, using their bodies as a canvas for personal expression.

This type of peaceful activism is framed around individual protest, and the clash of environment, body, and fashion becomes the act of dissent. Sapeurs and sapeuses transition from passive participants in a world they don't often control to actively owning their own narrative, granting themselves membership to an exclusive club of haute couture fanatics. Joining them in embracing this postmodern dandyism are stars like rapper Andre 3000, NBA player James Harden, and actor Michael B. Jordan, all of whom model how Black men can be architects of their own style and image. As the world has seen in the Black Lives Matter movement and in the 2020 protests specifically, tolerance for Black men being represented in a one-dimensional, stereotypical way has worn very thin. Sapeurs challenge the viewer to see a whole, vibrant person, echoing the idea that "if you can see it, you can be it."

In his Fall 2020 line, British-Ghanaian designer Ozwald Boateng pays homage to sapeurs, dandies, and Black fashion icons with his Africanism collection. [**Fig.17**] Traditional prints, handcrafted beading, rich color, and precision tailoring become, as the Boateng brand describes, the "embodiment of a continent's history, culture and style."[11] Now an established part of the deep history of Black style, Boateng was the youngest tailor to have a shop on London's Savile Row, opening his doors in 1995 and continuing the tradition of sharp suits celebrated by the mods, the zoot suiters, and the rudeboys. His brand dresses celebrities and everyday lovers of fashion alike while reclaiming space for Black style, design, and craftsmanship in the traditionally white sphere of fine suitmaking.

Writer Monica L. Miller explores race, identity, and reclaiming in *Slaves to Fashion: Black Dandyism and the Styling of Black Diasporic Identity* (2009). It's hard to overstate how important this book is to studies of modern dress history. Not only does Miller reframe perspectives on Black dress and culture, she also places ownership of Black visual identity squarely in the hands of the wearer. By conquering fashion, Black dandies use their bodies and clothes to take control over their personal sphere. Miller writes, "Dandyism might productively be called not a weapon of the weak but a weapon of the stylin'…using clothing as a means to create new images and identities and revise them yet again."[12]

In his Return of the Rude Boy I photographic series, visual artist Osborne Macharia documents fashion shows across Kenya, this

Fig. 17 (opposite)
Ozwald Boateng Spring/Summer 2020,
Photographer: Jamie Morgan, Model:
Dennis Okwera

Fig. 18 (above)
Remember the Rude Boy_02,
photograph by Osborne Macharia, 2017

one in the Kibera slum as a tribute to a popular local tailor. [**Fig.18**] Using his signature Afrofuturistic style, bold colors, and attention to cutting-edge fashion, Macharia places his sitters against bold backdrops in his native city of Nairobi, allowing their clothes, hair, faces, and poses to stand out. Macharia describes his work as an "artistic re-purpose of the post-colonial African narrative" through African design and self-created identity.[13]

Through these twentieth-century examples, we have seen fashion as an ally to most major cultural, social, and political changes: the social reform of the 1930s, the political resistance of the 1940s, the gender revolutions of the 1950s and 1960s, the environmental activism of the 1980s, the diversity and inclusivity movement of the 1990s and 2000s, and the movement for racial equality in the 2010s. Fashion has helped humans pass codes to each other, break and remake social contracts, and thwart their enemies. While fashion is all about individuality and the intimate interplay between fashion designer and consumer, the next three chapters will dive into a completely opposing way of using clothes: uniformity. The Black Panthers, Mahatma Gandhi's peaceful revolution, the Protestant Reformation, and Japanese kimono all share a common thread. They all use clothes to conform, and in myriad ways: to protect, hide, stand out, surprise, provoke, and unify.

PART TWO

Unity for Change

CHAPTER 4

Conform to Survive: Strength in Numbers

"The arc of the moral universe is long, but it bends toward justice."

—*Martin Luther King Jr., 1968, quoting Theodore Parker, abolitionist minister, 1853*

Branding and image making are not new phenomena, merely attributable to social media—they have been around since the beginning of civilization. From the prehistoric cave paintings of Lascaux, France (early selfies), and Fayum mummy portraits of Egypt (first century CE versions of a Facebook obituary post) to post-COVID-19 celebrity TikTok dances, we depend on image making for our social survival. Our hair, makeup, clothing, accessories, cars, homes, families, pets, and, recently, technology have become our allies in visual communication with each other. How we conform to social rules and how we covertly get around them through clothing is the focus of this chapter.

Talk show hosts dissecting the social media zeitgeist have helped thrust Victorian economist Thorstein Veblen into the limelight again, 120 years after he wrote one of the most influential studies on clothing and society, *The Theory of the Leisure Class* (1899). Comedian Hasan Minhaj devoted an entire episode of his show *Patriot Act* to deciphering Veblen for new generations. John Oliver, Jon Stewart, and Seth Meyers have translated Veblen's dense academic language into tasty sound bites. The economist's work fascinates us right now because he decodes our needs for approval and "'social confirmation' which nothing but a considerable body of like-minded people can give."[1] We crave a social confirmation feedback loop, and protest movements function in the same way. Rebellion is a two-way street: rebels send out signals, the establishment reads them, sends signals back, and the rebels respond again.

The Theory of the Leisure Class was written to decode how the middle classes became a force to be reckoned with and how they used newfound Industrial Revolution wealth to create social status markers. Veblen ties together visual identity, money, and status as his framework for social interaction: "Our apparel is always in evidence and affords an indication of our pecuniary standing to all observers at first glance."[2] Or as Hasan Minhaj might say, "My Nikes are always on show. Everyone instantly knows how much I paid for them."

Veblen broke down our social behavior through dress into four facets (this chapter proposes a new fifth facet). Veblen started with "conspicuous consumption": think Marlon Brando and his band of rebel teen consumers in Chapter 1. Brando was the face of a generation wanting not only to buy a rock-and-roll motorcycle but also to do it wildly and conspicuously. And almost no one did "conspicuous leisure" better than Oscar Wilde, discussed in Chapter 2.

Conspicuous leisure depended on showing that you didn't have to do manual labor or, ideally, any labor at all. The goal was to show that you had enough time, money, influence, and power to focus on beauty and aesthetics rather than day-to-day subsistence.

Fashion wins the award for "conspicuous waste" in Veblen's book. In Chapter 3, we saw that Marie Antoinette voraciously consumed clothes to show her power, wasting yards of expensive silks, thousands of feathers, and lifetimes of artisan labor. In her case, waste was equated with the power and status that led to her execution by the French rebels. Finally, the punks can claim the fourth facet, "conspicuous outrage." Infuriating society, punks invested time and creative energy into their outrageousness, intentionally breaking rules and embracing anarchy.

My theory of "conspicuous frugality" is a new addition to Veblen's original toolbox—standing out by dressing down, dressing appropriately, dressing respectably. Miniskirts, Mohawks, and leather jackets were meant for outrage and shock but the frugal homespun cloth worn by Gandhi's nonviolent protesters was shocking in its rejection of Western colonial dress. And the

Fig.1 (left)
Coming to Jones Road Tanka #3: Martin Luther King, from Coming to Jones Road Part II by Faith Ringgold, 2010

Fig.2 (right)
Reverend Martin Luther King Jr., Selma, Alabama, March 1965

Fig.3

Early Freedom Riders (from left to right): Worth Randle, Wally Nelson, Ernest Bromley, Jim Peck, Igal Roodenko, Bayard Rustin, Joe Felmet, George Houser, and Andy Johnson. Richmond, Virginia, 1947

black monk's robes that Protestant reformer Martin Luther wore in Renaissance Europe were rebellious because of their restraint. By rejecting fashion, luxury, and extravagance, Martin Luther, Gandhi, and the freedom fighters featured in this chapter forged a new, discreet identity for their causes.

Phenomenal cultural shifts like Martin Luther King Jr.'s civil rights movement and Malcolm X's radical Black Power activism made appropriate, modest, and respectable dress a cornerstone of their revolutionary identity. Rejecting ostentation in their own personal style, these leaders developed a visual trademark that followers could embrace, interpret, and emulate. King and Malcolm X knew the power of media, photography, and television, and curated images of themselves and their families that were inspirational to their followers, and inescapable to their foes.

Wearing a suit can be just as powerful as refusing to wear one. In a glorious sartorial contradiction, the punks, nihilists, and aesthetes rejected suits as establishment wear, while King and Malcolm X embraced them—even though they were all fellow rebels. A tailored 1960s middle-class suit and tie conformed to the

Fig.4 (opposite)
Bunny Wailer (left), Bob Marley (middle), and Peter Tosh (right), Jamaica, ca. 1964

Fig.5 (above)
Bob Marley, Santa Barbara, California, 1976

norm and said, "I'm just as much of a citizen as the president; I dress the way he does, and deserve the same respect." Celebrated painter, author, and performance artist Faith Ringgold portrays King in his iconic dark suit, white collared shirt, and tie in *Coming to Jones Road Tanka #3: Martin Luther King* (2010). [**Fig.1**] This unique portrait uses acrylic mixed media on canvas framed by patchworked fabric inspired by Tibetan Tanka paintings.

In *Sex and Suits* (1998), dress historian Anne Hollander investigates the enduring appeal of menswear. By wearing a suit, she observed, leaders like King and Malcolm X forced the world to see them as men, rather than second-class citizens: "When all men wear a white tie and black tailcoat in the evening, the individual character of each man is made more important, not less."[3] Images of men and women locking arms and marching for civil rights toward armed law enforcement were made significantly more compelling because the clothes were similar, the faces unique and individual.

Conforming to 1960s dress codes for the march across Edmund S. Pettis Bridge in Selma, Alabama, King and fellow protesters wore their respectable Sunday best to embody dignity, reinforcing a positive visual image of Black individuals. [**Fig.2**] They were willing to put their lives, bodies, and identity on the line for their beliefs. "The suit remains the uniform of official power, not manifest force

Fig.6
A nun, Selma to Montgomery March, Alabama, 1965

or physical labor—it suggests diplomacy, compromise, civility and physical self-control," writes Hollander.[4] But as King marched in the rain, his tidy suit ended up wet and disheveled. Black-and-white images of the marches were front-page news, and a drenched King in a makeshift rain cover, sanitation worker cap on his head, expressed the drama and risk of that day.

In the summer of 1961, dressed in freshly pressed suits and ties, summer dresses, slacks, and blouses, sixteen men and women, Black and white, boarded public buses in the humid Alabama heat. Nowadays, this would be unremarkable, but it was unthinkable in the recently desegregated South. Despite being beaten, harassed, stripped naked, and jailed in squalid conditions, founder James

Farmer and fellow members continued riding so the federal government would be compelled to enforce a 1946 law that desegregated interstate travel in the United States. The original Freedom Riders, the first of whom began protesting in 1947 with Journey of Reconciliation founders Bayard Rustin and George Houser, grew to four hundred members by the 1960s. [Fig.3] The law in question was a 1960s ruling that travel across the United States would be desegregated. By dressing formally the Black Freedom Riders sought to portray themselves as full members of society. By dressing in the same attire and riding alongside them, the white Freedom Riders supported their Black counterparts in clothing and action.

Neat, hip, and tidy, three young musicians in cropped sharkskin suits, skinny ties, black loafers, and tidy Afros were the future of Jamaican Black music. [Fig.4] But it's almost impossible to recognize Bob Marley, Peter Tosh, and Bunny Wailer as styled by their record label, Studio One. Jamaica gained independence from Great Britain in 1962, and the music coming out of poor shantytowns became the soundtrack to a new, emancipated generation. But the grit, poverty, and oppression of daily life on the island wasn't marketable to mainland audiences. The clean-cut look was familiar, approachable, and consumer friendly, a way to market Black reggae, dancehall, rocksteady, and ska to white audiences.

Once white listeners were hooked on the music, Marley took his fans along on his metamorphosis into the "Lion in Zion," returning to his roots. Touring the world as the early 1970s dawned, he left behind the aspirational two-piece suit, cropped hair, and close shave. A self-styled visual icon for the African diaspora, Marley found inspiration in Ethiopian leader Haile Selassie (whose visit to Jamaica in 1966 electrified the country) and Rastafarianism. Uniting denim work shirts, soccer tees, patchwork bellbottoms, knitted Rasta caps, sandals, and dreads, Marley's counterrevolutionary look came to epitomize radical 1970s fashion. [Fig.5]

Perched on the sidewalk edge of a Montgomery, Alabama, street during the Selma to Montgomery March of 1965, a nun rests her feet, an armed National Guardsman looming in the background. [Fig.6] Rallying alongside Martin Luther King Jr. and traveling with the Freedom Riders, Catholic nuns and priests of all races marched in Selma, blessed peaceful protesters in Montgomery, and hosted church services for activists across the country. The conspicuous frugality of their black-and-white habits lent gravity to the cause, raising awareness within their own congregations and drawing in churchgoers who may not have otherwise joined the fight.

Malcolm X, who started his fashion trajectory wearing colorful zoot suits, made himself a hallmark of modestly dressed Nation of Islam style, with his slim 1960s single-breasted suit, pocket square, neatly trimmed hair, signet ring (emblazoned with the Nation of Islam crescent moon and star symbol), and "browline" eyeglasses (always a Sirmont frame in shades of brown, made by American Optical). Clothing was an efficient ally in rebranding the Nation of Islam identity in the 1960s. The religious group was founded in 1934 by Elijah Muhammad but gained prominence as a radical Black Power organization as the civil rights movement blossomed. A black-and-white portrait by legendary documentary photographer Eve Arnold shows Malcolm X sitting in worship with Muhammad's wife, known as Sister Clara, and daughter. [Fig.7]

The Nation of Islam attracted a collective of Black women who found freedom in sisterhood and religious community. These women wore long, plain white dresses and crisp white headscarves. These uniforms evoked a feeling of purity and piety that visually unified female members and created a sense of

community. This uniform, similar to a modern nun's habit, reinforced the Nation of Islam tenant that women should dress modestly, creating a culture of high morality and respect.

The original Martin Luther ushered in the Protestant Reformation in early sixteenth-century Germany, dissenting against the excesses of the Catholic Church. Garbed in unadorned somber black vestments, he publicly showed his disdain for the wastefulness of the Church. Both High Renaissance upper-class fashion and Church vestments in mid-1500s Europe were often luxurious, colorful, decorated, expensive, and wasteful. By removing decoration, color, and cost from his own dress and vestments, Luther made himself into a walking icon for those who could not read the doctrines of the Church on their own. Luther's brand identity was dissent through the simplicity of his monks' robes, as he joined the Augustinian order in 1506 at age twenty-three. A 1528 painting of Luther, by close friend and fellow Protestant Lucas Cranach, shows how Luther rejected the sixteenth-century

Fig.9 (left)
Mohandas Karamchand Gandhi with
his secretary, Frau Schlesin, and lawyer,
HSL Polak, South Africa, 1900

Fig.10 (below)
Mahatma Gandhi, London, September
12, 1931

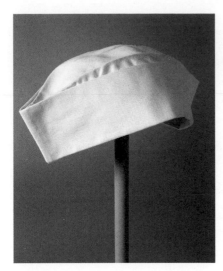

Fig.11
Topi hat, Kent State Museum Collection, date unknown

fashion of conspicuous waste. [**Fig.8**] Luther wears an untrimmed plain black flat woolen cap with his robe and a collared, pleated outer gown, signifying his status as a theologian and professor. Conspicuous frugality became Luther's weapon of resistance.

In 1900, at the dawn of a new century, a young lawyer in South Africa assembled his small team and had a photograph taken in front of his new shop. [**Fig.9**] The lawyer was Mohandas Karamchand Gandhi (later known as Mahatma Gandhi), and he would go on to practice law for twenty years before transforming into the iconic global leader we know him as now. Gandhi grew up wearing the tunic and soft pants of traditional Indian folk dress, but during his education in late Victorian England, Gandhi learned his way around a fitted men's suit, complete with waistcoat, starched collar, cravat, and bowler hat. When it came to elevating his cause to a global level in the 1920s, Gandhi rejected Western dress and returned to the traditional Indian unbleached cotton known as khadi cloth.

By dressing down and returning to traditional garb, Gandhi turned the convention of wearing Western clothing in India on its head. Instead of Western dress as a sign of modernity and progress, as the British had framed it, Gandhi saw it as a sign of colonial control and loss of national identity. He learned to spin thread on a wooden wheel (a *charkha*), and his followers also took up the craft of weaving natural handmade fabric, pairing it with modest sandals. Gandhi's message of a self-sufficient India, free of colonial rule, was visually represented by this elegant and modest patriotic uniform. In her 2019 book *Crafting Dissent*, Hinda Mandell writes that "khadi is simultaneously an artifact of material culture, an instrument of visual rhetoric, and a practice designed to communicate dissent and foster political participation."[5] So while British soldiers wore full Western military dress to suppress civil unrest, Gandhi's peaceful disobedience countered with a head-to-toe Indian visual identity. [**Fig.10**]

Topping off the new Indian identity was the topi hat, also made of khadi cloth, which was shaped like an envelope and easy to make and wear. [**Fig.11**] Mandell emphasizes the profound importance of this simple cap: "British authorities banned individuals from wearing the hats in government offices, courtrooms, and on college campuses, prompting additional acts of civil disobedience and increased opposition to the colonial regime."[6] By banning the topi hat, the British government threw fuel on the fire—the topi became more potent as a symbol of the struggle for self-rule.

Fig.12 (above left)
Men's Confederate shirt, worn by
Edwin Gilliam Booth Jr., 1863

Fig.13 (above right)
Men's shirt set/loungewear, 1950s

Fig.14 (left)
Girl's kimono (*Haregi*), Japan,
1940–41

Fig.15
Boogaloo arrest in Graham, North Carolina, June 27, 2020

Gandhi's Indian self-rule movement used cloth in elemental form, undyed and natural. A recent book dedicated to textile history by Kassia St. Clair, *The Golden Thread* (2018), tracks how fabric has permeated every corner of our lives: "The production of cloth and clothing has always been of great importance to the global economy and its cultures. Cloth gave humanity the ability to choose their own destiny."[7] Revolutionaries like Gandhi and his followers added another weapon to their arsenal by printing, dyeing, and embroidering fabrics, handkerchiefs, and home goods.

Slogans, phrases, images, and even maps have been printed on textiles in the service of political protest and propaganda. On display at the Imperial War Museum in London are 1940s silk day dresses recycled from Allied maps, while the American Civil War Museum permanent collection in Richmond, Virginia, holds an unusual artifact from American political history: a burgundy wool band-collared shirt, printed with tiny crossed Confederate flags. [**Fig.12**] Writes Jacqueline M. Atkins, "Propaganda textiles can provide a way to explore cultures on an intimate level, one that taps into thoughts, hopes and dreams, as well as general ideas, attitudes, and beliefs."[8] After the American Civil War started in 1861, Yankee manufacturers in the North churned out propaganda fabrics for both sides, ironically printed on cotton grown by slave labor in the Confederate South.

Profound cultural shifts are also documented in this girl's kimono from World War II. [**Fig.14**] A part of the Axis powers, Japan wove Nazi imagery into its daily dress: bombers, battleships, patriotic flags, soldiers, national monuments, and cultural symbols appeared on traditional Japanese clothing. Combined with traditional images of birds, waves, mountains, fish, flowers, and clouds, the propaganda motifs desensitized the general public to wartime. The kimono, already a breathtaking, centuries-old canvas for graphic design, morphed into a militarized government messaging system. Political symbols invaded the secular, private world of the home, carried on the backs of Japan's citizens.

Poolside Palm Springs parties, Florida vacations, and breezy road trips showed how far removed the post–World War II United States was from the devastation experienced in Europe and Japan. *Mad Men*–style advertising agencies glamorized modern cars meant for the open highway, mid-century homes meant for entertaining, and clothes meant for leisure. All this was, of course, meant for a heteronormative lifestyle. The tanned lifeguard and swimmer printed in bright colors on a casual men's shirt set

Fig.16 (above)
White nationalist Richard Spencer,
Washington, DC, June 25, 2017

Fig.17 (left)
National Socialist Party poster,
Germany, 1932

DRESSING THE RESISTANCE

alluded to gay sex, but only for those who could read the unspoken messages—covert textile prints sent secret signals to those within marginalized groups. [Fig.13]

Earlier on, similarly covert images were woven into turn-of-the-century American advertising campaigns. Illustrator J. C. Leyendecker perfected a glossy, dramatically lit graphic style, using his romantic partner, James Beach, as his model and inspiration for the handsome, dashing, hypermasculine Arrow Collar Man. Arrow manufactured men's underwear, detached collars, and tailored shirts. The ad campaign, showing perfectly groomed men wearing tailored shirts, socks, and underwear, ran in most major magazines in the United States, with the majority of the population unaware of its double meaning. Leyendecker crafted illustrations for many products, but the Arrow campaigns subversively wove a homoerotic gaze into the pages of early twentieth-century magazines. Leyendecker's male models existed in a refined, stylish advertising universe: they traded subtle glances across a crowded opera foyer, snapped the garters on their silk socks while dressing, and lounged on couches, deep in conversation with a male friend. Before gay men were legally allowed to live their lives in the open, they could live secretly through the fantasies of Leyendecker's illustrations.

Hiding in plain sight, but also loaded with hidden messages, the "boogaloo blouse" may win the prize for 2020's most surprising protest garment. The Hawaiian shirt, long worn by islanders and tourists alike, became the covert dress of the alt-right through convoluted internet wordplay. A material-culture artifact in itself, the iconic Hawaiian shirt is a hybrid of traditional Polynesian patterns and 1950s rayon leisurewear and had been enjoying a new life as the casual summer shirt of cool liberal millennials when it was swiftly co-opted. Brands like Tactical 5.11, a weapons and ammunition website, hawk camp shirts printed with floral motifs and warships, cheerfully advertising that "the Tropi-Camo Shirt offers the ability to blend into the crowd at your favorite equatorial destination or stand out at the weekend's BBQ."[9] Similar to the Nazi flags printed on Japanese kimonos, images of war and patriotism like retro biplanes, submarines, machine guns, and national flags are disguised within boogaloo blouses, intermixed with typical Hawaiian shirt motifs like desert islands and hibiscus flowers. [Fig.15]

Another staple of the Western male wardrobe has been similarly repurposed for the alt-right cause, precisely because of its entirely neutral quality. The plain white short-sleeved polo shirt, paired with basic beige chinos, has shifted from classic American casual wear to alt-right uniform. To the horror of brands like Fred Perry and Ralph Lauren, the piqué tennis polo, a symbol of elite leisure and sport, has been subverted. In a 2017 news photo, a well-dressed man is flanked by a group of clean-cut followers in matching polos and khakis. [**Fig.16**] At first glance, this could be any well-dressed businessman marching up the steps of a building. But this is Richard Spencer, running up the steps of the Lincoln Memorial after an alt-right freedom of speech rally in 2017. The president of the National Policy Institute, which described itself on its now-banned website as "at the forefront of alt-right activism," Spencer is the peacock at the forefront of this new clean-cut image-making campaign, complete with uniformed acolytes who complement but don't overshadow his style.[10] He wears tailored, expensive suits, matching ties and pocket squares, and crisp white shirts, branding himself as an alt version of a dandy.

A chilling Nazi propaganda poster from the 1930s features a strong, virile Aryan male shoveling away immigrants, wearing the same nondescript white shirt and khaki trousers that Spencer's followers are dressed in, minus the metal swastika belt buckle. [**Fig.17**] Additionally, recent photographs from the Charlottesville riots show screaming counterprotesters in matching white polos and Hitler-esque haircuts, sporting the aqua triangle of ethno-state group Identity Evropa on their left breast.

White supremacist figurehead Andrew Anglin also urged members to reject the militant skinhead look in favor of tailored clothes and groomed hair on his website the Daily Stormer, encouraging neo-Nazis to reform their image if they are to attract younger, millennial converts:

> *I cannot stress the point hard enough—I'm hitting italics again—we need to be extremely conscious of what we look like, and how we present ourselves. That matters more than our ideas. If that is sad to you, I'm sorry, but that is just human nature. If people see a bunch of mismatched overweight slobs, they are not going to care what they are saying.*[11]

Anglin continues on to give detailed sartorial advice to his followers, urging them to head to the gym, lose weight, and focus on their appearance. Anglin is a part of a larger movement fashioning a new look for the alt-right, rejecting stereotypical visual symbols

Figs. 18–22 (clockwise from top left)
Kekistan symbol, othala rune symbol, Identity Evropa symbol, 1488 hate symbol, and Blood Droplet symbol. Illustrations by Gwyn Conaway

like white supremacist tattoos, trashed jeans, slovenly T-shirts, and ungroomed hair.

Three interlocking triangles called the "valknut" gained notoriety when the QAnon "shaman" was photographed storming the US Capitol Building on January 6, 2021. Covered in an array of tattoos that are popular with pagan cultures but have been unfortunately co-opted by white supremacists, protester Jake Angeli's shirtless torso featured the Norse triangles, Thor's Hammer, and the Tree of Life. He completed the look with face paint and topped it off with a toy-store Viking helmet trimmed with fur. The Proud Boys, Oathkeepers, QAnon, and many other groups all identified themselves with T-shirts, hats, patches, badges, flags, symbols, and colors on that day. The outlandish costumes at the Capitol insurrection may have seemed humorous at first, but they were simply a distraction from a more sinister, subtle way of communication. The most dangerous individuals at the Capitol building that day would have been flying under the radar in the most incognito clothes, allowing the more flamboyant rioters to be the distraction.

Also at the Capitol were flags emblazoned with the "Kekistan" logo, an anarchist internet meme combining a Kelly-green frog called Pepe, an Egyptian god of chaos, and a cross iconography with a block letter *K* arranged on a white background. [**Fig.18**] These symbols, made into badges and patches, become easily purchased mass-market logos that signal allegiance to disruption and sedition that were added to military jackets, backpacks, and flak vests. As a banned symbol, even the swastika has been replaced by more subtle, abstract symbols of the alt-right. The Viking othala rune [**Fig.19**] now joins the swastika as a National Socialist Movement flag symbol, while a simple blood droplet [**Fig.22**], similar to a red comma, symbolizes the bloodshed of ethnic cleansing. As mentioned above, an aqua color and simple triangle motif was chosen for the Identity Evropa emblem. [**Fig.20**] Finally, the symbol of dice is a coded reference to 1488 in hate-group numerology. [**Fig.21**] To rebrand the alt-right, its leaders have focused on understated, covert design theory to conceal their members: a tiny red comma tattoo on your arm flies under the radar, while an inverted Christian cross on your neck does not. Aqua, black, bright green, red—colors play a crucial role in protest symbology—and that's exactly what we'll explore in the next chapter.

CHAPTER 5

Rainbow Warriors: Color Revolutions

"Color is a power which directly influences the soul."
—*Wassily Kandinsky,* Concerning the Spiritual in Art, *1914*

Humans have a complex, emotional relationship with color, making it a potent tool in protest movements. Like clothing, color is nonverbal but full of nuance, and can be decoded without language. In 1914, artist Wassily Kandinsky dedicated over half of his seminal book, *Concerning the Spiritual in Art*, to the language of color. Kandinsky ties the ethereal properties of color to what he calls a "purely physical impression": color acts on us in both an aesthetic and physical way.[1] Consequently, cultures have long-standing connections with color symbolism, rejecting some colors and celebrating others. This deep connection means resistance movements throughout history and across the globe have united and amplified their presence with color.

Color is simultaneously unifying and dividing—it is full of contradictions. In China and India, for instance, white is reserved for funerals, while in the West, for weddings and baptisms. And even among the endless variations of hues, tones, and shades, the ultimate contradiction of black and white inspires a unique design language. Tuxedos, the habits of nuns and priests, the robes of the Ku Klux Klan, and the costume of the Protestant Reformation all use the starkly contrasting palette of black and white to create visual harmony.

Throughout the ancient world, textiles and dyes were costly, difficult, and time-consuming to make. Color implied luxury: only the rich could afford the rare dyes and hours of labor it took to create a royal purple or a cardinal red. As a result, an elaborate system of rules, known as sumptuary laws, developed to determine which social classes could wear which clothing colors—sometimes, violations were punishable by death. In ancient Rome, you could identify a senator or a slave on the street by the colors they wore. In a 1562 statute, England's Queen Elizabeth I forbade anyone but the royal family and certain nobles to wear purple silk or cloth of gold; the colors crimson, red, and blue were strictly regulated; and a dizzying array of furs, velvets, woolens, and embroidery were reserved for royal use. Peasants, in many countries, were identifiable by their stark lack of color. Members of the working class wore clothes made from what grew naturally: mud-brown sheep's wool, beige linen, tan straw, and dark brown leather.

Color lies between creativity and science: it evokes emotions, sparks ideas, and inspires the spirit, as Kandinsky observed, but is created through chemistry and industry. In 1856, William Henry Perkin accidently invented synthetic dye while trying to create a chemical version of quinine. Suddenly, scientific progress meant that ordinary citizens had access to a kaleidoscope of cheaper dyes. And since sumptuary laws had largely died out in the seventeenth century, lifting the restrictions on wearing certain hues, the lower and middle classes could finally dress in the color of a king. We now take for granted that we can walk into any store and select a T-shirt or socks from a rainbow of color choices—technology and innovation have democratized color. The right, the left, peaceniks, anarchists, and religious conservatives can all equally harness color for a cause.

White

Democratic congresswomen channeled the suffragettes when they wore white to stand in solidarity with women's rights movements during the 2019 and 2020 State of the Union speeches. Not plain, sterile lab-coat white, but a myriad of stylish, confident variations on a white dress code. One person in white can make a fashion statement. Hundreds in white can signal a movement. The original suffragettes, marching in the early 1900s for women's voting rights, used white (accented by green, purple, and black) to create a startling tableau against the dark, coal-covered buildings of major cities across the United States and England. Hard to clean and easy to get dirty, white epitomized leisure, wealth, sport, and seaside resorts during Victorian times. As women in white marched through crowded streets and were arrested, the fabrics they wore were blank canvases on which stories of struggle—in dirt, blood, and sweat—could be told.

Kamala Harris wrapped all the meanings of suffragette white into one glorious silk-satin pussy bow for her 2020 vice-presidential acceptance speech. As the first woman and woman of color to become the US vice president elect, Harris knew that every detail of her speech, appearance, and tone would become part of history. Owning the heritage and symbolism of the moment, she wore a white tailored pantsuit with a coordinated blouse knotted at the neck with a soft bow that honored the style legacy of Hillary Clinton, Angela Merkel, and Margaret Thatcher. During her speech, she spoke directly to the citizens of the future, saying, "While I may be the first woman in this office, I will not be the last, because every little girl watching tonight sees that this is a country of possibilities."[2]

Red

Red is an imperial color in many cultures, and its status reflects its rarity. Before aniline dyes, pure red pigment was, and still is, harvested from tiny cochineal insects. In movies, red is used sparingly for dramatic effect: in the movie *Schindler's List* (1993), the red coat worn by a young girl walking through a gray landscape helps the audience track her to her death. Spanish rebels in the 1930s used bright red handkerchiefs to signal each other. And even Charles Darwin brought color into his scientific work, tucking a copy of *Werner's Nomenclature of Color* under his arm for his research voyage to the Galapagos Islands in 1831.[3] Abraham Gottlob Werner's color dictionary is an eighteenth-century taxonomy of 110 colors; in 1814 painter Patrick Symes added swatches to the original showstopping color names like "Hyacinth Red," "Veinous Blood Red," "Chocolate Red," and "Arterial Blood Red."

In modern-day South Africa, polarizing Marxist-Leninist agitator Julius Malema leads the Economic Freedom Fighters wearing bold red berets, safety helmets, and coveralls. His red jumpsuit honors common laborers and the spilled blood of working-class people, fitting since red is the color of blood, love, and emotion. A dandy dresser from an early age, Malema harnesses the power of clothing both in his personal and private life. However, it may also end up being his Achilles' heel as controversies surface about his passion for designer shoes, astronomically priced watches, and bespoke suits.

DRESSING THE RESISTANCE

Pink

Fig. 3 (opposite)
Sampat Pal Devi, Uttar Pradesh, India,
November 5, 2019

The story of pink is the story of color and gender. A dilution of the royal-red dye revered by the ancient Aztecs and European royalty, pink was confidently worn by upper class Western men from the sixteenth century until the Industrial Revolution, notably in Giovanni Batista Moroni's 1560 portrait, *The Gentleman in Pink*. For Marie Antoinette it was a power color, while fashion designer Elsa Schiaparelli (see Chapter 3) created a rebellious shade called "shocking pink." Before the twentieth century, pink could be worn by boys and blue by girls, but a post–World War II marketing tactic rebranded pink as a girl's color.

In the twenty-first century, every gender gets a shot at wearing pink. Rapper and LGBTQ+ icon Lil Nas X (who wore a studded bubblegum-pink leather cowboy outfit, complete with chaps and ten-gallon hat, to the 2020 MTV Video Music Awards), sports figure James Harden, and actor Jason Momoa have reclaimed every shade of pink for the twenty-first-century man confident in his gender identity. Jayna Zweiman reclaimed the color for the Pussyhat Project, describing how she used it to "flip the feminine-associated color as something strong," and marveling at how suppliers across America ran out of pink yarn once pussyhat knitting went viral.[4]

For the Gulabi Gang (*gulabi* means "pink" in Hindi), the color represents anger spurred into action. Armed with pink-painted bamboo sticks that match their fuchsia saris, the gang is not opposed to using violence in the service of justice. A self-styled vigilante gang, the group's half-million members organize to defend women's rights in India, especially focusing on poorer, unrepresented women from the lower social castes.

Orange

Orange is the color that the human eye recognizes most easily. No wonder then that the Guantanamo Bay prison jumpsuits were manufactured in screaming industrial-safety orange. Greenpeace used the bright tone to raise awareness for the Arctic 30, a group of international activists arrested and held by Russian forces for two months. Ukraine's Orange Revolution adopted the color for its 2004 civil resistance, and in 2007, political Buddhist monks wearing robes in shades of deep orange marched nonviolently in Myanmar for regime change. Thousands of monks flooded the streets, and the Saffron Revolution was born. Pro-democratic monks exiled in Thailand continued the protests, and in this photo from 2009, they carried enormous banners printed with opposition leader Aung San Suu Kyi's portrait in Bangkok.

The robes date back 2,500 years to Gautama Buddha himself, who adopted them from the already ancient Hindu religion into which he was born. Early cloth for robes was scavenged or accepted as donations by the monks who had renounced worldly goods and embraced simplicity. They dyed the cloth with many natural spices and plants: the saffron stigma of the crocus flower, turmeric root, curry powder. A wide range of reddish, orange, and yellow tones were inspired by colors of a burning flame, representing truth. In 2011, political monks in Myanmar and abroad propelled Aung San Suu Kyi to the presidency. But in early 2021, a military junta arrested Suu Kyi and took power amid protest rallies and violent crackdowns, and once again the world may see Buddhist monks filling the streets in shades of saffron.

Yellow

Fig. 5 (opposite)
Umbrella Movement protests, Hong
Kong Island, August 18, 2019

This barefoot protester walks in the rain, holding his simple yellow umbrella. Up to a hundred thousand marchers in Hong Kong joined the 2014 Umbrella Movement for free and independent elections. Protests lasted seventy-nine days, and the umbrellas were at first a utilitarian solution, protecting the citizens who filled the streets from being sprayed with tear gas by police. As time passed, the sea of yellow caught in aerial photos became emblematic of the movement.

Yellow umbrellas have become a lasting symbol of Hong Kong's social justice causes and were carried in 2019 marches for the fifth anniversary of the movement's inception and in subsequent 2019 protests against a proposed change in Chinese extradition laws. Sculptures, graphic posters, and murals featuring the distinctive yellow umbrellas are now part of Hong Kong's urban fabric as enduring civic art pieces.

Both umbrellas and the color yellow have a long history in China. While ancient Egyptians may have been the first to develop handheld papyrus sunshades, a folding umbrella was invented in China around 500 BCE, and at the same time yellow was strictly a royal color, banned from everyday use. Writer and journalist Victoria Finlay devotes a glorious 448 pages to shades and tones in *Color: A Natural History of the Palette*. She notes that "in Asia, yellow is the color of power—the emperors of China were the only ones allowed to sport sunshine-colored robes."[5] The Umbrella Movement spoke truth to power, claiming the forbidden shade for the common people.

DRESSING THE RESISTANCE

Green

Fig.6 (opposite)
Election rally, Tehran, Iran,
June 9, 2009

Green evokes nature, calm, and health but also jealousy, sickness, and envy. As the color of hope, green marked the 2005 Lebanese Cedar Revolution, and a few years later in Iran, the 2007 Green Movement used a bright shade to galvanize the country in social change. One-hundred-foot-long Kelly-green fabric banners were carried through the streets by protesters wearing green body paint, home-made scarves, and fabric wraps. Flashing a peace sign, this protester, wearing a black chador (a semicircular piece of cloth worn over the head and closed under the chin) and with her wrist wound with green fabric, holds a photo-copied image of Mir-Hossein Mousavi Khameneh, the leader of the liberal Green Movement, over her face.

The chador has its own resistance history: worn for centuries in Persia, it was forbidden by progressive ruler Reza Shah in 1936. Iranian clothes were Westernized to symbolize progress and modernity, with men wearing three-piece suits and fedoras and women exposing their legs and arms in 1930s-style day dresses. Only in 1980, during the Iranian Cultural Revolution, did the chador reappear as religious groups began severely restricting women's rights.

Blue

Fig. 7 (opposite)
Kalakan Health Clinic, Afghanistan,
February 23, 2003

Uniformity can play a dual role in a resistance movement. Identical clothing can make individual members of a group completely anonymous and the group highly visible as a form of protection against an oppressive regime. In Afghanistan, performing a seemingly basic personal task, such as attending school, can result in arrest because civil liberties for women and girls are extremely limited. Afghan women wearing blue burkas have been quoted as saying that they feel safer when they are in a group of women who are uniformly covered from head to toe because the anonymity of the burka shields their identity.

The Taliban cannot identify the offending woman and certainly cannot arrest every woman wearing a burka; therefore, the garment grants women the liberty to move through daily life and, perhaps, perform small acts of dissent (like going to a secret school) without punishment. To these women, protest is found in a garment that to the Western eye may appear restrictive but which itself permits a form of freedom and offers protection.

Purple

Fig.8 (opposite)
International Women's Day rally,
Mexico City, March 8, 2018

For the past several years in Mexico, on International Women's Day, women have stayed home, excusing themselves from work and giving nannies and housekeepers the day off. Showing what "A Day Without A Woman" would look like, Mexican activists used their absence to make a statement. Donning bright purple, long a color of feminist movements, women painted their faces and followed the strikes with celebratory, music-filled marches.

Fifty years earlier, in the United States, the phrase "lavender menace" was used by writer Betty Friedan to describe lesbians in the women's rights movements. The name was embraced by a 1970s collective of militant lesbians, who took on the color to represent gay rights. Hand dyeing their T-shirts to shades of lilac, mauve, and orchid and stenciling them with the words "Lavender Menace," they agitated for gay representation within the women's movement.

Long before purple became a color for feminist movements, it was a color of extreme luxury, power, and conspicuous waste. In ancient Lebanon, near the city of Tyre, where a natural purple dye was discovered, ten thousand tiny native *murex purpurea* shellfish were needed to make just one gram of dark purple dye.[6] Roman emperor Julius Caesar excluded everyone but himself from wearing a full purple toga (the toga picta or toga purpurea), and this tradition lasted hundreds of years into the Byzantine era. Caesar's consuls were allowed only a purple stripe on their toga praetextae. With this rich history, purple becomes a powerful color to reclaim for equality and equity.

Black

Black is a stark, dramatic, austere choice for dissent. From Renaissance princes to twentieth-century goths and from long-standing martial arts traditions (medieval samurais wore navy and dark brown as well as black for nighttime maneuvers) to Western funeral traditions, black has never been shy. During the 2018 Golden Globe Awards, actresses wore all black to support the budding #MeToo movement. Black Lives Matter elevated the color to a viral level in 2020, as hundreds of thousands of citizens across the world demanded an end to systemic racism. Black T-shirts with bold white lettering gave the movement an iconic visual identity and gave followers a simple, straightforward way to join the cause.

During the 2020 COVID-19 pandemic, international sports superstars added #BlackLivesMatter masks to their arsenal of awareness-raising activist tools. The only Black NASCAR driver, American Bubba Wallace, raced a Black Lives Matter car on the Atlanta Speedway, wearing a #BLM mask and T-shirt. The same year, Lewis Hamilton became the most successful driver in Formula 1 race history. Still the only Black Formula 1 driver, he wore #BlackLivesMatter masks and T-shirts, while his competitors supported him by wearing "End Racism Now" tees as Hamilton knelt during the United Kingdom national anthem, raising his fist in a Black Power salute.

Rainbow

Fig. 10 (opposite)
Presidential swearing-in ceremony,
Warsaw, Poland, August 6, 2020

Greenpeace named its flagship boat the Rainbow Warrior, while LGBTQ+ communities use the rainbow to symbolize the inclusion of all genders, sexualities, races, and beliefs. Rainbow flags were carried at LGBTQ+ rights marches as 2020 saw waves of protests across the world. And in defiance of Polish President Andrzej Duda's homophobic comments in 2020, female members of the Council of Ministers coordinated their fierce fashions on the Parliament steps to support equity. Each member dressed in a color of the rainbow, posed for group photos outside, and then seated themselves in rainbow formation on the parliament floor. Playing against the uniformity of the navy and dark gray suits of male Parliament members and their president, each woman joyfully harnessed color for activism. This is twenty-first-century female-power dressing with a message, echoed thousands of miles away by the United States congresswomen in white. Power and dress frame the next chapter as well, as we move on to explore the military and the subversive ways protest groups deconstruct the uniform.

CHAPTER 6

Military to Militant: Join the Club

"**Complete conformity of dress means uniform, not fashion.**"
—*Michael Carter,* Fashion Classics from Carlyle to Barthes, *2003*

The military exists through power: who has it, who doesn't, who wants it, who doesn't. The potency of the military depends on showing force, intimidation, and dominance; uniforms are designed to make a soldier look bigger, tougher, and stronger. Across continents, throughout time, cultures have endowed military forces with an almost mythical status. Stories of warriors like Boudicea, Achilles, and Genghis Khan are passed down through generations. Military dress is the visual language of these cultural myths.

Uniforms encode visual cues that differentiate between friend and foe and identify "the other." Rebellions throughout history have adopted the visual language of battle dress for precisely this reason. Uniforms separate resistance fighters from regular citizens in the public space and readily distinguish opposing rebel groups. Easy-to-spot blue shirts worn by 1930s Spanish counterrevolutionaries, for example, "brought a new visibility in political mobilization: the cadres were on the street, openly agitating, demanding to be seen."[1]

This quote from *Fashioning the Body Politic: Dress, Gender, Citizenship* (2002) could easily apply to contemporary direct action on the streets as well. In the wake of the 2020 presidential elections in the United States, two radical political groups clashed in public battles. Antifa supporters wore all black, some disguising their faces with bandanas, some in flak jackets and black helmets. Agitating against fascism, neo-Nazis, and racism, Antifa activists went head-to-head with the Proud Boys, the alt-right white supremacist group, in the streets of Washington, DC. The Proud Boys appropriate a militia style: utilitarian BDU (battle dress uniform) jackets, wraparound tactical sunglasses, camo baseball caps, semiautomatic weapons. Curator and art critic Gabi Scardi describes the uniform as a "collective garment." Both groups used message tees as a collective garment to unify their causes—easy to distribute, easy to throw on in the midst of protest, easy to show whose side someone is on.

Subversion also plays a key role: take a conventional piece of clothing from those in power and undermine its traditional meaning—you've got a new weapon for dissent. The most straightforward way is to take the military uniform out of the barracks and straight to a protest. Vietnam vets campaign for peace by wearing their old uniforms—the change simple but profound. Something as easy as flipping the American flag patch on your camo jacket upside down can be a potent metaphor for flipping the power dynamics of society.

Fig.1 (left)
Dakota Access Pipeline protest, Oceti Sakowin Camp, Cannon Ball, North Dakota, December 5, 2016

Fig.2 (above)
Che Guevara, Havana, Cuba, 1961

In a 2016 photograph, an unnamed individual standing in the snow in Cannon Ball, North Dakota, wears a hooded camo-patterned parka and shows their dissent with an inverted American flag. [Fig.1] When local tribes learned that the American government was planning an oil pipeline that would skirt the Standing Rock Sioux tribal lands and disturb sacred burial ground, Native and non-native activists flooded the area, setting up spiritual protest camps like Sacred Stone and Oceti Sakowin. Riding in on horse-back, the neighboring Standing Rock Lakota people and other tribes peacefully joined the Sioux in opposing the lack of consulta-tion with tribal government, and some stayed for months. So far, the protests by the "water protectors" have had an impact: in 2020, the Dakota Access Pipeline project was shut down for review.

Che Guevara, the Argentinian rebel leader of the Cuban Revolution, took a four-pocket khaki military uniform, meant to be tidy and orderly, and twisted it into a dusty, disheveled, and unabashedly hip symbol of the resistance. [Fig.2] The same ingre-dients, different taste. Guevara, with his signature shaggy hair and scruffy beard, has become the quintessential image of a rebel. Simply changing the context of the uniform destabilizes its mean-ing. Since his death in 1964, he has achieved immortality, appear-ing on T-shirts, bumper stickers, hats, and graffiti stencils. College students have taken up Guevara's look as they experience their own process of rebellion and growth, and it has become so ubiqui-tous that a young musician walking down the street in Lebanon, Gambia, or Peru might be seen wearing a four-pocket khaki jacket, unaware of the symbolism of resistance on their back.

Mass movements use a different visual language from the image of the lone rebel. There is safety in numbers and power in repetition. As *GQ* reporter and author Bill Dunn writes, "Uniforms helped to engender a feeling of pride in one's country and one's cause—charging into battle with similarly dressed compatriots uni-fied by fast-beating hearts and minds."[2] During the 2014 Revolution of Dignity, when Ukrainian freedom fighters protested government inaction on EU membership, they did so carrying bats and sticks, wearing any and all safety gear they had. [Fig.3] The protesters were mirroring the fully armed pro-government Ukrainian police with their own jumbled, homemade version of riot gear, highlighting the inequity between the two opposing groups.

The Black Panthers showed that you didn't need to sacrifice style for a serious cause. They developed an infamous military-inspired look that was easily replicated by regular people shopping

at common American stores, like J. C. Penney or Sears. Members rocked a now-iconic look to back up their politics: black beret, leather jacket, black turtleneck, and dark trousers, which could easily be adapted for women with the substitution of a skirt. The Panther look also embraced contemporary 1970s fashion: leather jackets, fitted jeans, natural Afros, and sleek turtlenecks. In a 1969 photo, taken at a courthouse rally, the Panthers are caught in a rare informal moment, dancing and relaxing in their matching combat boots and black sunglasses. [Fig.4]

The beret, turtleneck, and heavy black paratrooper boots were all originally used by militaries around the world. The felted wool beret has the longest history, worn as a worker's cap since the time of ancient Greece—one was even found in the walls of a Renaissance building, left behind by a fifteenth-century laborer. The beret transitioned into military wear as British troops added it to uniforms in their colonial regiments. The turtleneck started as a utilitarian solution for sailors—it kept the rain out and warmth in. Sportswear trends in the twentieth century propelled it into fashion, and its relaxed elegance framed a 1970s Afro perfectly.

Finally, in Western cultures, thick leather boots were the legacy of ancient Roman gladiators, Viking marauders, and medieval Crusaders. Native American tribes perfected an easy-to-make, one-hide boot: just cut a leather sole from the skin of an animal, sew it to the rest of that skin, and lace it over the leg, as high as you need.

Fig.3 (above)
Pro-European protesters, Kiev, Ukraine, January 22, 2014

Fig.4 (overleaf)
Black Panther Party members, New York City, May 1, 1969

DRESSING THE RESISTANCE

For horseback-riding Native warriors, the boots provided crucial protection from the underbrush. The Black Panthers absorbed all this military precision and heritage, working it into their highly structured organization. When the *New York Times* reporter Gerald Emanuel Stern interviewed two Panthers in 1970, he marveled that their "shoelaces were tied identically, forming precise bows along the left side of each foot. Soldiers, I thought, ready for inspection."[3]

Huey Newton understood the potency of visual communication when he was photographed by Blair Stapp in his Black Panther uniform, with a gun, spear, African shields, and a zebra skin while seated in a rattan peacock chair. [Fig.5] Newton founded the Black Panther Party for Self Defense with Bobby Seale, and while they took inspiration from military dress, they also channeled international revolutionary movements, like Marxism and Leninism. Eldridge Cleaver, a party leader, posed Newton in the chair, surrounded by masks and a zebra pelt, aware that it would reference African warriors.

Revolutionary groups are virtuosos of using graphic design, art, and clothing to craft a unique identity that the public can easily digest and follow. The Panthers wrapped their uniforms into an image-making universe that included the *Black Panther* newspaper, the prowling panther logo, youth groups complete with school-style uniforms, and a sophisticated range of posters, banners, badges, and buttons. The film *Black Panther* (2018), directed by Ryan Coogler, pays homage to this iconic Huey Newton image. In the movie, Chadwick Bozeman, as King T'Challa, sits on a sci-fi version of the rattan "throne" when meeting with his intergalactic council of leaders.

Honed to perfection by centuries of war, uniforms are the ultimate example of form following function, incorporating only the most useful and necessary elements. But there is beauty in spare, utilitarian design. A long tradition of insignia, badges, and pins create legitimacy, conformity, and order within ranks, while camouflage, color, and technology keep soldiers protected. No wonder, then, that military innovation is often absorbed into civilian culture. High-tech fabrics like neoprene, Tyvek, nylon, and rayon were developed as replacements for costly materials needed for silk parachutes and rubber scuba suits; the modern wristwatch was born in action during World War I as a portable compass and timepiece. Modern fashion is full of crossover combat gear: duffle coats, leg warmers, culottes, T-shirts, three-button Henley tees, bucket hats, and aviator sunglasses.

As war moved from the ground to the air in the early twentieth century, an iconic jacket evolved alongside rapid aviation innovation. The interiors of World War I planes were freezing, spurring the 1920s development of a shearling flight jacket in Britain. As World War II approached, pilots wore a fitted leather version of the flight jacket (also called the bomber jacket) that provided warmth in high altitudes, blocked drafts with ribbed cuffs and collar, and was light and streamlined in a cockpit overcrowded with gadgets. A marvel of form and function, the pockets for pens, maps, and supplies were placed strategically on the jacket, and a distinctive orange lining made a downed pilot easy to spot.

During World War II, military textile innovations made nylon and other performance materials widely available, and the nylon bomber jacket was born. First made in the United States by Dobbs Industries, the A-Series bomber could be made in any color or camouflage pattern. It segued into fashion on the backs of Hollywood stars like James Dean in the 1950s, transitioned to

Fig. 5 (left)
Huey Newton, Black Panther Minister of Defense, 1968

Fig. 6 (right)
Cesar Chavez's union jacket, 1993

skinhead counterculture style in the 1970s, and is now worn as a casual, unisex alternative to the suit jacket, gaining iconic cinema style status on the back of Ryan Gosling in the 2011 movie *Drive*.

An MA-1 style nylon bomber jacket, housed in the Smithsonian Museum object collection, was worn by farm labor activist Cesar Chavez. [Fig.6] From his early life as a migrant worker, Chavez understood the trials and tribulations of the laborers he fought for as leader of the United Farm Workers union, along with Dolores Huerta. Chavez, in simple worker's clothes, straw hat, and jeans, became the face of the struggle against exploitation. Chavez customized this all-black bomber jacket just like fighter pilots did: he adorned it with patches and badges. In the air force, the jacket was a canvas for military insignia and ranking; for Chavez, it carried the symbols of his nonviolent movement. The patch on the jacket reads "Farmworkers AFL-CIO" and features the black and red abstract graphic of an Aztec eagle, designed by Chavez's brother. A red button with white writing reads "NO GRAPES," alluding to the 1965–70 consumer grape boycott for fair wages. "Cesar Chavez" is written in simple white lettering (just like a soldier's name badge) over the left breast.

While uniforms add legitimacy to self-appointed social groups, these groups can just as easily represent oppression as they can freedom. In 1961, a neo-Nazi group called the American Nazi Party created faux-military uniforms to present a cohesive message to the American public. These uniforms, designed by Party members, reinforced leader George Lincoln Rockwell's white supremacist symbology, along with the "Hate Bus," a vehicle covered in white supremacist text that drove through the deep South. [Fig.7] Lincoln Rockwell and his followers traveled and staged rallies, provoking police into impounding the bus and disbanding the group. Rockwell styled his "troops" in khaki trousers and collared shirts, swastika armbands, and polished black shoes, referencing smart military dress.

The contrast of identical neo-Nazi uniforms to the soft, knitted sweater and draped skirt of this lone female counterprotester makes for a mesmerizing photo. [Fig.8] The woman in the image is Tess Asplund, who was on her way to work, in Sweden, when she saw men from the Nordic Resistance Movement marching in their matching black pants, crisp white shirts, and dark ties. She placed her body in front of the men in a spur-of-the-moment decision, raising her fist in the gesture of Black Power. Social media made this image go viral, and Asplund became an everyday folk hero.

Fig.7
George Lincoln Rockwell (far right) and
his American Nazi Party, May 22, 1961

Folk heroes have been the inspiration for numerous reinventions of military uniforms in revolutionary history. Taking peasant dress and traditional motifs and clashing them with military dress, Leon Trotsky refashioned his Red Army as a visual symbol of 1920s Marxist ideology. Unlike Asplund's spontaneous protest, it took intentionality, time, money, and factory labor to re-create the uniforms of a major national army. "It was not by chance therefore that the military uniform of the Red Army was reminiscent of Medieval Russia," writes Lidya Zaletova in the 1987 book *Revolutionary Costume*.[4] Reaching back to early Slavic folk dress, the designs referenced fifteenth-century murals. A line drawing of Red Army uniforms from 1918 shows designs for the *pastrano* caftan with an asymmetrical neckline, pointed Byzantine-style hats, and a summer jacket called the *bogetyrka*. [Fig.10] By World War II, all the remnants of the nouveau folk uniform had disappeared, as had the revolution. But as Communism rose in Russia and China, new solutions for broadcasting political ideals appeared.

Fig.8
Tess Asplund, Borlange, Sweden,
May 2, 2016

Communist iconography and classical ballet collided when young female dancers, on pointe and carrying guns, performed across China in the 1960s and 1970s. The People's Liberation Army reinforced its campaign of nation building and propaganda with performances of *The Red Detachment of Women*, a military ballet with a dash of sexuality. [**Fig.9**] The costumes were a clash of folk dress and military influence and featured the *shanku* (a tunic paired with matching shorts or trousers). Author Antonia Finnane details the evolution of Communist nation building performance in her book *Changing Clothes in China: Revolution, History, Nation* (2007): "The Red Detachment of Women, with its chorus line of skimpily-dressed women soldiers, won young red hearts all over China, and entrenched the iconic status of army uniform among them."[5]

While the military has historically been an arena of masculinity, a feminine perspective occasionally sneaks in, as in the case of Irish rebel hero Constance Markievicz, who invented a military uniform in service of her own revolution. Legend has it that she gave fashion advice urging stylish women to buy a revolver and designed the Citizen's Army uniform for Ireland's 1916 Easter

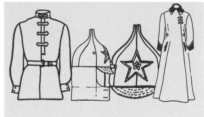

Fig.9 (top)
The Red Detachment of Women,
National Ballet of China, 1972

Fig.10 (bottom)
Designs for Leon Trotsky's Red Guard
uniforms, 1918

Rising. Seen in street demonstrations, she carried a cigarette in one hand and a gun in the other. Her Citizen's Army uniform was a dark green wool jacket, men's breeches, and dashing hat with a feather. Markievicz was born to an Arctic explorer, married a wealthy Ukrainian artist, and, after an early life as a landscape painter, dedicated herself to Irish nationalism. [Fig.11] After founding the paramilitary boys training organization Fianna Éireann, she spent the rest of her life using her own fortune to fund various republican causes, joining hunger strikes and dying penniless.

It is possible that Markievicz may have modeled herself on one of the original female cross-dressing military rebels, the legendary Joan of Arc. [Fig.12] Burned at the stake in 1431 at only fifteen years old, Joan had a vision that she should lead the French army against the English; to gain the trust of Charles VII, the soon-to-be French king, she wore male military armor. During the late-medieval times and into the Renaissance, European military armor was made of heavy plates bolted together. Underneath, some soldiers wore chain mail and, to protect themselves from the sharp metal, a doublet and breeches of padded canvas. Joan would have worn this incredibly heavy uniform as she rode into battle. Denying her the right to be burned in garments of her own choice, her English captors decided that she should go up in flames wearing a simple women's hemp tunic, her head shaved clean. Now a French martyr and hero, she died as a revolutionary.

The English suffragettes, ironically, used Joan of Arc as their symbol of insurgence when they began publishing a newspaper called the *Suffragette*, in 1912. The Women's Social and Political Union (WSPU) led the charge in agitating for women's voting rights, and one of the newspaper's covers, with graphic design by Hilda Dallas, uses the three suffragette colors of purple, green, and white to frame a modern, twentieth-century Joan of Arc. [Fig.13] This new warrior is layered in iconic pieces of European military dress history: the Renaissance metal plate armor, a white medieval tabard with "JUSTICE" lettered across the chest, seventeenth-century Cavalier gauntlet gloves, a Byzantine pointed helmet. Carrying a green WSPU banner in one hand, a heavy sword in the other, this Joan of Arc is an exemplary mash-up of martial dress. Seventy years later, gender equality is still a battlefield.

Fashion disrupter Rudi Gernreich designed clothes as a commentary on the world around him. As an openly gay German immigrant, the maverick designer was an outsider, which gave him a unique perspective on American 1960s culture. Gernreich

expected his designs to shock and provoke. The Fashion Institute of Design and Merchandising Museum in Los Angeles houses the Rudi Gernreich Archive, including a 1970 knitted, beige four-pocket military ensemble, complete with a safari turban and aviator glasses, which takes the uniform and transforms it into a symbol of women's liberation. [Fig.16] Looking back on his career during a 1985 presentation at the Smithsonian Institute in Washington, DC, Gernreich commented, "I did the military look in the late 1960s because some designers were making Scarlett O'Hara clothes, which I thought was an insult to women when they were becoming totally equal to men."[6]

More recently, the Combat Paper project teaches military veterans to recycle their old uniforms into pulp through the art of papermaking. Founder Drew Cameron leads workshops during which vets unleash their own creativity as they heal from PTSD or, conversely, honor their military service. They unravel "the story of the fiber, the blood, sweat and tears, the months of hardship and brutal violence that are held within those uniforms."[7] Cameron calls his practice peace work: "to transform the uniform into paper, to remake it, to change all previous relationships to it into your own, and to change your relationship to the memories brought up

Fig.11 (left)
Constance Markievicz, carte de visite, Dublin, 1916

Fig.12 (right)
Portrait of Joan of Arc, from *Les Poesies* by Charles D'Orleans, fifteenth century

Fig.13 (opposite)
Poster for the *Suffragette* newspaper, cover by Hilda Dallas, 1912

by it—how you were treated, the things that you've done or seen
or done to others—that's what Combat Paper is interested in."[8]
In a photo of the project, Cameron strips himself of his uniform,
holding it in his hand almost meditatively. [**Fig.14**] Documenting
the process becomes part of the papermaking, and the images
transcend seamlessly from realism to art as they are printed on
the handmade sheets. [**Fig.15**]

Finally, humor in military dress can be a potent tool for commentary. Magnum photographer Dennis Stock, who spent the
1960s documenting nonconformist culture in California, took the
photo *Pacifist Demonstrating in Santa Monica* in 1968. [**Fig.17**] In
it the antiwar protester wears a kitschy revamp of military dress
with comically exaggerated medals and a white captain's hat with
a toy fighter jet flying over the brim. He devalues and disrespects
his ill-fitting military uniform by amateurishly adding household

Fig. 16 (opposite)
Safari ensemble by fashion designer
Rudi Gernreich, Resort, 1970–71

Fig. 17 (above)
The California Trip by Dennis Stock,
Santa Monica, California, 1968

sewing basket items, like rickrack and ribbon, and holds a fake
newspaper prop with a headline that reinforces his sartorial
choices: "WAR IS IN VERY BAD TASTE." The look crosses over
from military uniform to costume parody, turning his protest into
a street performance. In the next chapter, we'll explore how costume can transcend the ordinary and turn a regular Santa Monica
sidewalk into a stage.

PART THREE

Beyond Clothing

CHAPTER 7

Costume and Rebellion: Acting Up, Acting Out

"I'm just trying to change the world, one sequin at a time."
—Lady Gaga, 2008

A costume is a tool of performance: it transforms the world around it into a stage. People for the Ethical Treatment of Animals (PETA) supporters have dressed as whales, chickens, tigers, bunnies, pigs, and packages of raw meat in an effort to grab the spotlight. Tea Party populists in red, white, and blue pilgrim-style dress have rallied for lower taxes and stricter immigration. The Occupy and Anonymous movements use masks just as a Shakespearean performer would have done, to create drama and tell a story. A costume is different from clothing, uniform, or fashion because it takes the wearer out of their ordinary persona. Inside a costume, the wearer becomes a character transcending their daily life and empowered to break social codes and expectations.

World War II French Resistance fighters used costumes to conceal their identity, escape arrest or abuse, and camouflage themselves on the streets. The opposite approach is to be overt and bold: climate action group Extinction Rebellion stages elaborate, haunting costume parades to commandeer public spaces, showing how dressing up helps demonstrators stand out on a busy sidewalk. Wearing a costume doesn't require much money, just imagination and a little effort, making it accessible, cheap, and creative.

Humans have carved out space for all kinds of entertainment since the very beginning of society, including rituals, dance, theater, music, film, and video. Costumes, masks, accessories, and props flourished alongside the developing art forms. Freedom fighters can grab endless opportunities for expression through costume, from perfectly planned flash mobs to spontaneous riots. The rebels in this chapter must choose either safety or risk, going incognito or perhaps ending up on the evening news. For instance, we look at how enslaved Black communities in the South in the early days of the United States developed a rich carnival and parade tradition to mask hidden dissent. Or the Yes Men, who use large-scale public hoaxes to achieve maximum disruption. Modern day LGBTQ+ movements uplift their communities through drag, cross-dressing, and camp performances.

Sequins, exuberant sexuality, magic, and anarchy collided in 1970s San Francisco when the Cockettes burst onto the scene. Performing at midnight during hippie movie screenings known as the Nocturnal Dream Show, the Cockettes powered their queer rebellion with androgynous thrift-store-costumed spontaneity. The head of the Cockettes was its charismatic founder Hibiscus (born George Irving), shown wearing fur, makeup, a golden beard, and a turban festooned with fruit. [Fig.1] In the 2002 documentary

The Cockettes, film director John Waters describes the group as "hippie acid freak drag queens."[1] Blurring the binary lines between public and private, male and female, performance and mundane life, Hibiscus and his troupe jumbled social codes as fluidly as they jumbled their costumes.

San Francisco's infamous Sisters of Perpetual Indulgence burst on the scene as a loose band of community activists in 1979, joining

Fig.1
Hibiscus, *Luminous Procuress*
film still, 1971

Fig.2
Sisters of Perpetual Indulgence,
Seattle Pride Parade, 1995

Easter Sunday parades dressed as joyously twisted nuns. [**Fig.2**] Self-described on their website as "a leading-edge Order of queer and trans Nuns…[who] use humor and wit to expose the forces of bigotry, complacency, and guilt," they have developed into a worldwide phenomenon, with one nun, Sister Roma, raising over $1 million for LGBTQ+ charities.[2] These jubilant costumes also carry a serious message: hate crimes against gay and trans individuals happen often, and living out in the open and freely choosing what you wear can be perilous.

Performance artist Leigh Bowery deployed latex, masks, paint, makeup, foam, household objects, and towering heels to disrupt conservative norms, distorting his body into a living art piece. In a 1989 photograph by Matthew R. Lewis, Bowery is seated backstage, wearing a beaded crystal headdress, showgirl corset, and glittery platform shoes, with a tangle of yarn and thread at his crotch. [**Fig.3**] In the 1980s, Bowery turned his own infamous nightclub, Taboo, into a personal catwalk, creating look after gender-bending look for his polysexual audience.

Expanding into the fine-art space, Bowery installed himself in the Anthony d'Offay gallery in London in 1988, in a room of

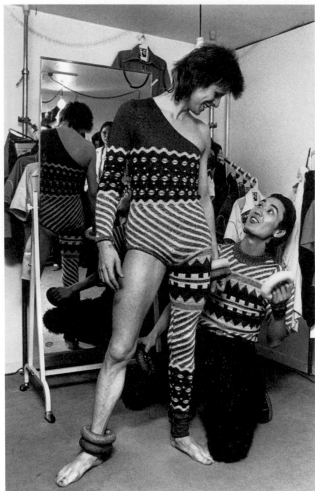

mirrors and plexiglass, allowing audiences to observe him. While his looks were purposely outrageous, nightmarish, and grotesque, Bowery's dissent with everyday culture went far further than drag. A person of larger stature, Bowery rejoiced in featuring his body despite the judgment of others, even posing nude for painter Lucian Freud. Bowery identified as gay, but he married his best friend Nicola Bateman in 1994, involving her in his photographs and performance art until his death from AIDS complications several months later. A recent retrospective of his work and a posthumous Spring 2020 street-wear collaboration with cult skate brand Supreme introduced him to a new generation and gave visual voice to postmodern queer culture.

Performance, gender, and flamboyance all collided when David Bowie wore Japanese designer Kansai Yamamoto's knitted jumpsuit onstage in 1973. Yamamoto was experimenting with reenvisioning the human form, creating pieces that distorted the body. Bowie used these fashions to elevate his image and transcend gender boundaries. He invited Yamamoto to watch a show, and

Fig. 3 (left)
Leigh Bowery by Matthew R. Lewis, 1989

Fig. 4 (right)
David Bowie stage costume fitting with Kansai Yamamoto by Sukita, 1973

BLOOMER COSTUMES OR WOMAN'S EMANCIPATION.

Fig.5

Bloomer Costumes or Women's Emancipation, lithograph, ca. 1853

a long collaboration was born. A 1973 photo by Sakita, a longtime Yamamoto creative collaborator, documents Yamamoto in the fitting room with Bowie, the two of them wearing matching knitwear and nurturing a subtle, covert type of protest, one that promotes individual choice and suggests a new way of looking at masculinity and dress. [**Fig.4**]

American early feminist Amelia Bloomer and her followers created a visual symbol of women's suffrage by adopting the dress of men as a kind of "suffrage costume." Known as "bloomers," these provocative pants were an innovative resistance garment. [**Fig.5**] Although the first suffrage parade occurred in New York in 1910, Bloomer had already invented the Turkish-inspired trunks in the 1850s, a time when women risked being socially ostracized, fired from jobs, and censured by their families for swapping their skirts for trousers. In many cultures, men wear what is equivalent to the skirt or sarong, but for American Victorians, this type of cross-dressing was revolutionary. The bloomer was born and became a lasting visual symbol of women's liberation. The public outrage they caused helped spark a movement, and after a long fight, women began to win the right to vote in the United States.

Rather than breaking boundaries with innovative postmodern, futuristic costumes, as we saw with the Cockettes, Bowery, and Bowie, contemporary Women's Marchers went back in time, channeling their inner suffragette. In a 2018 news photo, an activist steps onto the streets of London wearing a replica of a typical period look of the 1910s—a fitted jacket, a full-length skirt, a sash

Fig.6 (above)
March 4 Women activist, Westminster,
London, March 4, 2018

Fig.7 (right)
Emmeline Pankhurst arrested by police
outside Buckingham Palace, London,
May 21, 1914

150

of green, white, and purple, a Gibson Girl hairstyle, and a wide straw hat—while carrying a picket sign proclaiming "Deeds Not Words." [Fig.6] Putting a costumed twist to a rebel look, the outfit grabs attention by standing out from the average pedestrian in a hoodie, jeans, AirPods, and Adidas sneakers on their way to the tube station.

Emmeline Pankhurst, founder of the women's suffrage movement, would have been proud. A black-and-white photo card shows Pankhurst in 1914, being lifted off the ground, while still protesting, by a uniformed London policeman outside Buckingham Palace and surrounded by concerned male chaperones. [Fig.7] She wears the quintessential late-nineteenth-century Victorian fashion of a proper lady: a dark ankle-length dress with white blouse, hat, veil, feather, black stockings, and neat pointed shoes. As Cally Blackman, coauthor of the book *A Portrait of Fashion* (2008) points out, since suffragettes were "haunted by the stereotypical image of the 'strong-minded woman' in masculine clothes, pebble-thick glasses and galoshes created by cartoonists, they chose instead to present a fashionable, feminine image."[3]

Twenty-five years later, the image of a strong-minded woman in masculine clothes was a fraction easier for the general public to accept, thanks to the catalyst of early twentieth-century cross-dressing. Post–World War I underground lesbian clubs in Germany, the androgyny of artist Romaine Brooks, and gender-nonconforming aesthetes and writers, like Peter Gluck, wiped away the traditional feminine dress codes of Victorian times. A Smithsonian National Portrait Gallery retrospective of Brooks's work featured a 1924 oil portrait entitled *Una, Lady Troubridge*. [Fig.8] Una wears exquisitely tailored menswear, a dashing monocle, and a black cravat, her face framed with a sharp flapper bob. At the time, men were arrested for engaging in same-sex relationships, and it was inconceivable that most women would have the autonomy to choose their sexual partners. Brooks inherited vast wealth, which put her in a unique position to build exactly the life she and her entourage desired, able to dress in traditionally masculine styles but protected from arrest, abuse, or ostracism by a circle of money and privilege.

In 1930, Gary Cooper and Marlene Dietrich starred in *Morocco*, directed by Josef von Sternberg for Paramount Pictures. [Fig.9] In her first American film, Dietrich was dressed by costume designer Travis Banton in a men's tuxedo, white tie, and top hat. [Fig.10] The intimate and intense relationship between star, director, and

Fig.8 (opposite)
Una, Lady Troubridge by Romaine
Brooks, 1924

Fig.9 (left)
Marlene Dietrich, *Morocco* film
still, 1930

Fig.10 (right)
Marlene Dietrich, *Morocco* costume
rendering, costume design by Travis
Banton, 1930

costume designer gives movies a unique role in covertly changing
culture, and this was clearly the case in *Morocco*. Art historian
Anne Hollander (whose work will be explored further in the next
chapter) notes in her seminal book *Seeing Through Clothes* (1973):
"Ordinary clothes automatically become extraordinary on the
stage or screen."[4] Moviegoers watched, electrified and shocked,
as Dietrich kissed another woman on the big screen, a moment
amplified by costume and dramatic lighting. "Dietrich is smudging
the defining boundaries of her femaleness," writes Stella Bruzzi,
who describes this scene as an empowering event that pushes forward a woman's own agency in becoming a whole person, outside
of society's expectations.[5]

The Anonymous social-justice movement uses a pop-culture
film reference to simultaneously conceal individual identity and
unify its members. While providing a disguise, the Guy Fawkes
masks from the 2005 film *V for Vendetta* (costumes designed by
Sammy Sheldon) were used as a simple tool: Anonymous protesters in masks used their bodies to create a theatrical image that is
instantly recognizable but individually unidentifiable. [**Fig.11**] In
Anonymous marches from Spain to Turkey, the Guy Fawkes mask
was a nonverbal signal. As social media grows in importance in

how rebellions are broadcast, these movements will continue to need portable symbols that can be tweeted, texted, posted, and Instagrammed.

Anonymous activist group the Guerrilla Girls also uses costume to shake up the art world. Wearing Halloween-style gorilla-head masks with modern street clothing, a tradition that started when, as struggling artists they didn't want to face discrimination for speaking up, they hid their identities but not their voices. Disguised as gorillas, activists appeared at art openings to highlight sexism and racism in the art world. The Guerrilla Girls website mysteriously states: "We are everywhere. We could be anyone."[6] Throughout the 1980s the group created some of the most iconic protest posters of the twentieth century, now collected in volumes with pithy titles like *Bitches, Bimbos and Ballbreakers* (2003). Still active, it is fitting that they are now artists in their own right, achieving cult status in the graphic design world and beyond.

Even before the Emancipation Proclamation of 1863, Black consumers had been creating their own unique cultural identity through music, entertainment, literature, and performance—they just had to do it covertly. As the shackles of slavery receded slowly, generation by generation, the creative spirit of Black performers grew stronger and stronger. In profiling the blues icon Bessie Smith, the *New York Times* writer Daphne Brooks solidified the connection between art, design, and dissent: "Pop music was transformed by a people whose musical innovations were—and

Fig.11 (left)
Ageing Anonymous by Florian Belmonte, 2016

Fig.12 (right)
Josephine Baker, Folies Bergère costume, 1927

Fig.13
Madame Leroy by Fabiola Jean-Louis,
Rewriting History series, 2018

remain today—the manifestation of a brutal, centuries-long, blood-soaked struggle to be regarded as human in the West."[7]

Tastemaker, performer, activist, and philanthropist Josephine Baker was at the epicenter of this cultural movement in the early twentieth century. Not just performance costumes but also everything about her lifestyle—her everyday clothes, fashion, cars, furniture, parties, and a castle in France—became a part of her lifelong narrative to heighten visibility for racial harmony. Baker began her career in vaudeville in the 1910s, found herself swept up in the Harlem Renaissance, and toward the end of her life became an activist, speaking alongside Martin Luther King Jr. during the 1963 March on Washington. In between, Baker adopted children from thirteen different countries and traveled worldwide with her "rainbow tribe," all the while living life as a celebrity in France, performing, and starring in films.

In an iconic image, Baker wears a crystal-covered banana skirt, jewels, and pearls for a Folies Bergère show in Paris. [**Fig.12**] The

Fig.14 (left)
Dressing for the Carnival by Winslow Homer, 1877

Fig.15 (right)
Solomon Northrup by Frederick Coffin, 1853

synergy between music, art, culture, and rebellion was perfectly framed by the Harlem Renaissance. Baker took this spirit to Paris in the early 1920s and shaped how Black entertainers could raise awareness for racial equality with their star power. Like Smith and Baker, writers and musicians Duke Ellington, Cab Calloway, Ma Rainey, and Langston Hughes celebrated Black lives in and around the Harlem neighborhood in post–World War I New York.

Picking up where twentieth-century activists like Baker left off, Fabiola Jean-Louis elevates Black and brown women's bodies through formal but thoroughly modern photographic portraits. Crafting exquisite garments entirely from paper to attire women of color and placing her sitters in traditional seventeenth- and eighteenth-century Western art poses, Jean-Louis reclaims portraiture for a new generation. While able to stand alone as fine-art pieces, the images also conjure a powerful narrative of identity and memory. A pigment print entitled *Madame Leroy* (2018) shows a serene, contemplative woman wearing a fine mid-eighteenth-century dress, the bodice made from newspaper collage. [Fig.13] In the center of the bodice is a small 3D jewel box with a tableau of a male slave hanging from a tiny tree blooming with delicate pink flowers. The elegance of the portrait clashes with the brutal death represented by the tiny figure; Jean-Louis brings history to life, tethering the past enslaved life to the ongoing struggles for equality of Black and brown women.

Slave-era carnivals and festivals were bright spots of relief and community gathering in an otherwise relentless six-day plantation work rotation. Winslow Homer painted this group of slaves in 1877, portraying earlier Southern festivals that featured parades and exaggerated costumed characters. [Fig.14] A woman with thread and needle puts the finishing touches on a colorful red and yellow costume as adults and children in plain everyday dress look on. Carnivals like the Christmastime Jonkonnu (the subject of the Homer painting) in the South and Easter holiday Pinkster in the Northeast, along with Sunday churchgoing, were some of the only times slaves were allowed to replace their daily work clothes.

Writer Steeve O. Buckridge has studied Jamaican rebellion through dress from the 1830s to the twentieth century and writes extensively about slave festivals and carnivals. "During the performances, language, dress and the body became agencies for empowerment, ridicule and resistance."[8] Jonkonnu and Pinkster celebration costumes were complex, imaginative, and thriftily made with supplies from the plantation and, along with Sunday-best church outfits, wove expressions of personhood into an otherwise dehumanized world.

Enslaved men and boys were given a rough set of shirt and trousers, homespun on the plantation from hemp or coarse cotton, as worn by Solomon Northrup in an engraving by Frederick Coffin from 1853. [Fig.15] Northrup wrote the autobiography of his legendary escape from slavery after being captured as a free man, taken from his family, and enslaved. He is portrayed here not in the middle-class Victorian three-piece suit he would have been accustomed to wearing but in the "plantation suit" and straw hat slave owners would have issued to him. It's been said that the older brothers would wear in the new stiff clothes of their younger brothers until they were no longer painful on the skin, giving the clothes back to them when they were comfortable enough to wear. Women and girls were given a simple ankle-length work dress, crowned with a head rag, usually a scavenged square of cloth that kept out lice and kept hair clean. To save on the cost of dyes, these clothes were plain in color or sometimes tinted with indigo blue, which was cheaply imported and used for work wear.

Finally, costumes also allow rebels to use tongue-in-cheek humor to catch attention. In the first image, a group of anti-LGBTQ+ counterprotesters stand under a banner that reads "Homosexuality is Sin! Return to Jesus!" [Fig.17] Standing in front of a dividing line of police in screaming-yellow safety coats, a bearded man with long brown hair participates in the 2017 Seoul Queer Culture Fest. Dressed as Jesus in a white robe and long red sash, he carries a sign that reads "I'm Cool with It," subverting the counterprotesters' message with love and a cheeky smile. Sometimes humor, satire, and parody can diffuse tension, allowing passersby to chuckle as they gaze and think about what the protester is communicating.

"Waging peace" through joy and satire is how grassroots organization CODEPINK operates. Clad in hand-sewn walkabout vagina costumes, some decorated with sparkles and sequins, CODEPINK activists at the 2012 Republican National Convention used playful shock tactics to bring light to serious issues. [Fig.18] The surprise of seeing an intimate body part made large and proud through costume can attract maximum attention. The name CODEPINK is a play on the United States government's color-coded terrorist-threat alerts, and the color pink unifies members as they stage street theater to promote peace, women's rights, and humanitarian causes.

Imagine the absurd sight of people in inflatable gray suits, wobbling around the edge of a barren desert landscape. [Fig.16] That's "laughtivism," or activism fueled by humor. Yes Men cofounder Mike Bonanno puts it plainly: "Not doing anything about climate change is even stupider than this costume."[9] The Yes Men revel in satire, parody, and staging bizarre stunts as they raise awareness for urgent environmental action. Bonanno and cofounder Andy Bichlbaum launched the Survivaball suits as a hoax, masquerading as Halliburton energy company representatives at a catastrophic-loss conference in 2016. These conferences gather world business leaders in seismic events and risk management, and they also hawk high-tech missile launchers and disaster innovations. Arriving armed with a fake infomercial about their new protective suit, the Yes Men handed out phony press releases, setting a $100 million price tag per suit.

As we have seen throughout this chapter, the basic act of dressing the body becomes an out-of-the-ordinary experience on stage, screen, and the street. Through performance, activists can normalize new societal rules, trigger cultural progress, and overturn thinking that quietly hinders emancipation. Costume is a great equalizer, used by the humblest of slaves and the wealthiest of socialites. And costumes are meant to get reactions, whether laughter, fear, revulsion, or curiosity, making them a protest tool that engages an audience and provokes them to feel. The magic is that anything can become part of a costume: a mask, a scrap of ribbon, a toy plane, a glittery platform go-go boot, or a bunch of plastic fruit. In the next chapter, scraps of ribbon, buttons, jewelry, accessories, and hats take center stage as we explore portable protest objects.

Fig.16 (above)
Yes Men Survivaball Suit, ca. 2009

Fig.17 (opposite top)
Robert Evans, an American photographer from Atlanta, Georgia, dressed as Jesus, Seoul Queer Culture Fest, July 2017

Fig.18 (opposite bottom)
CODEPINK protesters, Republican National Convention, 2012

CHAPTER 8

Portable Protest: Hide and Seek

"Emotional value—now that is a worthy goal of design."

—*Donald A. Norman*, Emotional Design, *2004*

Portable items of rebellion are small in size but not in impact. Common objects like a ring, a handkerchief, or a badge, combined with a personal emotional narrative, can function as a talisman and good-luck charm, a commemoration of an overcome trauma, or a reminder of a happy moment. Art history professor Anne Smart Martin elevates mundane goods to a metaphysical level in her article, "Makers, Buyers, and Users: Consumerism as a Material Culture Framework" (1993): "Material objects matter because they are complex, symbolic bundles of social, cultural, and individual meanings fused onto something we can touch, see, and own."[1] Most of us have an object like this in our lives, something that may not have monetary value but is nevertheless priceless. When tied to a broader social movement, these portable items can quickly become historical records of personal protest.

Like an ancient Twitter system, early cultures used accessories, such as hats, pins, jewelry, and amulets to broadcast information quickly. An accessory could become a viral real-time analog method of communication for a peasant, farmer, or serf who couldn't read or write. One hat might be an individual statement; many hats let rebels know how many allies they have on their side. Portable protest, therefore, is practical and functional but also highly personal. A bit of magic happens when we carry and use an accessory for a long time; it wears and tears in highly personal ways. A group of rebels wearing the same neck scarf or prayer beads will customize them differently, revealing a story of individualism. In the book *Emotional Design* (2004), author Donald A. Norman praises objects that have grown old gracefully, noting that "this kind of personalization carries huge emotional significance, enriching our lives."[2]

A simple, repeated image can enhance a budding movement, especially in the social media age. During Harvey Weinstein's 2019 New York City trial, women protesting rape and sexual harassment across from the courthouse flash mobbed in black mesh "blindfolds," dancing and chanting. [Fig.1] In the photographs, which went viral, the clothing was crucial: black and red garments, strips of net fabric cut and shared among women, many of whom were wearing a touch of bright red lipstick. The inspiration was a Chilean performance piece against femicide and rape called *Un violador en tu camino* (A Rapist in Your Path).

Waves of pink pussyhats filled the streets as Women's Marches kicked off around the world after the Trump inauguration in 2016. Also mentioned in Chapter 5, project cofounder Jayna Zweiman

Fig.1
Harvey Weinstein trial protest, New York
City, January 10, 2020

Fig.2
"Speak Truth" quilt by Katherine H.
McClelland, 2017

explains that people who couldn't go to the marches could still show up by knitting and donating hats, and that each unique hat could hold intimate personal stories written on a note tucked inside. With an easily distributable digital pattern (designed by Kat Coyle), Zweiman and Suh gave protesters a crowdsourced tool for their movement. Katherine McClelland worked her "Speak Truth" quilt, a self-portrait in her own pussyhat, after the January 2016 anti-Trump marches in Washington, DC. [**Fig.2**] Shadowed in the fibers of the quilt, the words "Speak Truth Show Love" are McClelland's commitment to energizing her politics and becoming an active participant in the struggle against hate. Spreading a message may have been made easier with the use of social media, but societies have used headwear and hats for collective action across millennia.

Knitting itself has been used as a form of resistance, with knitter-rebels cropping up throughout history. The French Revolution (explored in Chapter 3) saw organized bands of female market stall workers angry at the scarcity of food and a lack of support from the French monarchy. These women took to the streets, marching to the Royal Palace, demanding bread and respect. They were incorporated into the overall revolutionary movement until they were deemed too "unmanageable" by rebel leader Robespierre and his followers.

Fig.3
Les Tricoteuses Jacobines, Jean-Baptiste Lesueur, 1793

Fig.4 (top)
Bust of Attis, marble sculpture,
second century CE

Fig.5 (bottom)
French Revolutionary cap, Los Angeles
County Museum of Art, 1790

Upon being rejected, some stationed themselves near the Place de la Concorde guillotine in Paris and ominously knitted hats, sometimes using precise stitches in the headwear to encode the names of aristocrats sentenced to death, earning themselves the nickname *Les Tricoteuses* (The Knitters). [**Fig.3**] Modern knitters keep the tradition going with "knitbombing," or "yarnbombing," a craftivist way of showing dissent. Covering fences, bike racks, and street sign poles in knitting, crochet, and wrapped yarn transforms a public surface into a messaging machine. When disability rights advocate, comedian, and avid lifelong knitter Stella Young died in 2014 at thirty-two years old, knitbombing tributes cropped up along accessibility ramps and handrails across her native Melbourne, Australia.

The knitted pussyhat shape also has some famous ancestors. Ancient Rome saw slave rebellions throughout the Empire, particularly from 1–300 CE. Roman slaves granted emancipation were given a pileus (a soft, pointed wool or leather hat) to visually symbolize their freedom. Imagine a Roman city square full of newly freed pointed-hat-wearing former slaves, and you have the ancient version of the pussyhat. A Princeton/Stanford working group on ancient slavery patterns estimates that 15 to 25 percent of Italian inhabitants were slaves.[3] The cap became a symbol of freedom and has been immortalized in an ancient Roman marble sculpture of a young man named Attis. [**Fig.4**] Versions of this cap existed throughout the ancient world, including a similar Phrygian cap from what is now modern-day Turkey. Late-eighteenth-century France saw the rise of the bonnet rouge (red hat), also called the liberty cap and Phrygian bonnet, worn by the working class to show solidarity with the cause of the French Revolution.

In eighteenth-century France, red had already been a high-status hue for centuries, traditionally worn by the church and monarchy. Since ancient times, red dye was extremely valuable— it came from tiny marine insects and was difficult to harvest, and getting a deep red color in particular involved a labor-intensive process. Therefore, red textiles were a luxury, and the bonnet rouge became a symbol not only of protest but also of power. One variation of the bonnet rouge was called a bonnet de police because it was worn by the National Guard. [**Fig.5**] A tiny Phrygian cap is embroidered on the red band, and the hat itself is in the revolutionary colors of red, white, and blue, also known as tricolor. Rebels showed their allegiance to the cause with tricolor cockades, metal brooches, ribbons, lapel pins, and jewelry.

Fig.6
Asmaa by Mohammed Zaanoun, Gaza,
2019

Fig.7
Pussy Riot activists in front of the Kremlin, Moscow, January 20, 2012

Concealment and disguise are the chosen tool of another band of crusaders for women's rights: Pussy Riot. Wearing balaclavas, bright-colored clothing, and fishnet tights and playing their own brand of punk music, the group is a collective of anonymous members, although three of them (Maria Alyokhina, Yekaterina Samutsevich, and Nadezhda Tolokonnikova) shot to fame after being arrested for hooliganism and tried by the Russian government in 2012. The striking images of Pussy Riot standing on monuments and playing rock in churches are amplified by their performance costumes and anonymous faces. [**Fig.7**]

A dusty keffiyeh scarf gives both anonymity and protection against tear gas to Asmaa, a twenty-three-year-old woman from Gaza. [**Fig.6**] Since grassroots demonstrations known as the Great March of Return began in 2018, Mohammed Zaanoun has been photographing activists at the Palestinian territories' borders with Israel. The marches strive to raise awareness for Palestinians prevented from returning to ancestral lands and to agitate against Israeli blockades. Zaanoun describes how Asmaa, with the support of her family, refuses to give up her weekly visits to the border fencing despite the dangers: "She and her sister were suffocated by gas as they stood in front of the fence, but they quickly recovered and returned to protest."[4]

Fig.8
Illustration of Funmilayo Ransome-Kuti
by Gwyn Conaway

The keffiyeh winds a beautifully labyrinthine path through Middle Eastern politics. Originally worn across the Middle East by peasants as a traditional head covering, it was later appropriated by the Arabs in the 1930s fight for Palestinian freedom. Jane Tynan, writing in *Fashion and Politics* (2019), dissects how the keffiyeh shifted from being a guerrilla-fighter head wrap to a required urban uniform. The keffiyeh made guerrilla fighters obvious to the British, who invaded Palestine to quell dissent. "To resolve this problem, in 1938 the rebel leadership commanded all Arabs in urban areas to all wear the keffiyeh. While this made it impossible to know whom to arrest, the widespread adoption of the cotton headdress intimated that everyone in the country was a rebel."[5] During the 1970s, the keffiyeh transformed once again into a counterculture fashion accessory. Today it remains a global trend, detached from its political history but still symbolizing revolutionary struggles.

Continuing our global look at portable protest, African freedom fighters like Funmilayo Ransome-Kuti, the twentieth-century Nigerian political activist, also reclaimed headwear and color as a tool of communication and resistance. In an illustration by artist Gwyn Conaway, Ransome-Kuti, who was educated in England, wears her graduation mortarboard made from plain black fabric in a square flat shape (left), worn for centuries by Western scholars. [Fig.8] On the right, Ransome-Kuti is depicted years later when she began to wear traditional Yoruba dress, which reflected her Nigerian roots, having traded the angular mortarboard for an organic, softly draped head wrap in a bright yellow and green pattern.

With one powerful change in headwear, she showed her allegiance to the lower-class women working in the open-air markets of Nigeria, whom she taught to read and write through her Ladies' Club social movement. In 1977, Ransome-Kuti was thrown from a window in a raid by Nigerian soldiers and died of her injuries, leaving behind her world-famous son, Fela Kuti, who carried on her rebellion through his music. The head wrap is a bridge between two worlds, Africa and the United States. Ransome-Kuti's Nigerian head wrap has echoes around the world and across time, from slavery to modern day. "It is a tradition which continues today… when Black American women of all ages wear the head wrap for all manner of occasions."[6] Like Mahatma Gandhi's topi hat, which we saw in Chapter 5, headwear can transcend from the everyday to the extraordinary.

Another Black female freedom fighter, Queen Nanny, legendary eighteenth-century leader of the Jamaican Maroons, was believed to have hidden ammunition (and magic!) in her head wrap. Head wraps were worn to transmit messages and hide contraband from the white colonial conquerors in the Caribbean uprisings of the First Maroon War (1728–40). Queen Nanny led a band of escaped slaves who were living in the mountains and defending themselves from slave owners trying to recapture their "property." Queen Nanny has also been depicted wearing amulets on her chest, a traditional African practice. These amulets were considered magical and were a visual code for spiritual protection from the threat of recapture. Queen Nanny and her followers could have easily and swiftly removed and hidden their head wraps and amulets, quickly transforming from Jamaican Maroon rebels to slaves.

At that time in the Caribbean, slaves wore simplified Western dress in work-wear fabrics but adapted their clothes in many ways to accommodate the island climate and harsh living conditions. Through a coded language based on how the head wraps were tied, those involved in the rebellion could read hidden messages, unbeknownst to the colonialists. As secret-code transmitters,

Fig.9 (left)
Purse, FIDM Museum, 1824–27

Fig.10 (opposite top)
Civil Rights Marchers, Memphis,
Tennessee, March 29, 1968

Fig.11 (opposite bottom)
Occupy Wall Street activist, New York
City Supreme Court, November 5, 2011

these head wraps were a matter of life or death. Primary sources detail "shooting parties" during which white visitors to the islands would be taken out on expeditions, to hunt not animals but escaped slaves.

More recently, nineteenth-century suffragettes carried a change of clothes when they marched, so they could duck into a doorway and get out of their marching whites, purples, and greens and into a new look that would not be identifiable to the police. Suffragettes used fabric sashes, buttons, pins, and hat decorations to add color to and visually unify their marches, and these accessories could be hidden quickly in a bag. Some of the same women who campaigned for the vote also campaigned for abolition.

Fashion Institute of Design and Merchandising (FIDM) Museum curator Christina Johnson notes that "fashion is not just a matter of taste, but an instrument of profound social change."[7] A heartbreaking example of this is a purse from the FIDM Museum in Los Angeles, which shows how political a delicate silk handbag could be. [Fig.9] These bags were worn by middle-class abolitionist women who gifted them to their peers and to political figures of the day. One side of the purse depicts a slave woman, wearing only a white length of cloth, holding her sick baby. On the other side, written in perfect penmanship, is an abolitionist poem. Inside were pamphlets featuring slave-ship manifests, descriptions of historical events, and letters. Riding a tram in Boston or Philadelphia

170

in 1860, you might have seen a middle-class woman with this bag on her lap, read the poem, and decided to join the cause.

Elegant jewelry was also a favorite tool of the women's rights suffragette groups of the nineteenth and early twentieth centuries. The Holloway brooch, a metal and enamel pin given to women's liberation activists jailed at Holloway Prison in London, became a badge of pride for women who were awarded it. The pin was in the shape of a portcullis or jail gate and decorated with tiny metal chains and three triangles in the iconic colors of the British suffragettes. White stood for purity, green for hope, and purple for royalty.

Black men with placards draped over their bodies with the words "I Am a Man" became the heroes of the sanitation worker protests in Memphis, Tennessee, in 1968. [Fig.10] Each man had the same board with the same typeface, black lettering on a white background. Creating uniformity, these placards reinforced the sheer number of protesters and also gave them a cohesive visual identity. Uniforms can play completely opposing roles in a resistance movement: identical clothing can make members of a group anonymous as a form of rebellion, but it can also make that same group highly visible. This was not a use of decorative or stylish protest imagery worn on the body. It was matter-of-fact, blunt, and graphic and resonated strongly with the visual medium of black-and-white photography. In 2011, an unknown protester was photographed in homage to the sanitation workers, wearing an "I Am A Human" T-shirt while being restrained by officers during a series of Occupy Wall Street protests in New York City. [Fig.11]

Similarly, the "We Are the 99 Percent" movement used both uniformity, disguise, and graphic lettering to highlight how the top one percent of wealth in the world is owned by a very small number of people. Banding together with the Occupy Movement in 2011 to express dissent against economic inequality, the 99% campaign offered a brand identity ready to go viral: grab a piece of scrap fabric, a can of red spray paint, and a cardboard stencil, and you have a cheap and instant way to join the cause. The brainchild of Alex Weinshenker, 99% bandanas were churned out in an Occupy print shop in Los Angeles. Red stencils of "99%" on bandanas could both disguise the wearer and make all protesters look alike while functioning as a billboard for the uprising.

Art gallery worker Sarah Mason wore one at an Occupy march in Los Angeles and unwittingly became the 2011 face of protest. [Fig.12] It was an ordinary day when Mason left her Occupy tent

Fig.12 (opposite)
Occupy protester Sarah Mason
by Ted Soqui, 2011

encampment in LA and joined yet another rally. Photographer Ted Soqui's casual snapshot of Mason's face was remixed by graphic artist Shepherd Fairey, landing on the cover of *Time* magazine. "The Protester" was named *Time*'s 2011 Person of the Year, and Sarah Mason became the poster child for the Occupy and 99% movements simultaneously.

Just a simple scrap of fabric with a message, armbands have been an effective method of communication for many movements. The French National Front, a far-left communist contributor to the French Resistance in World War II, used hand-embroidered cotton armbands to visually distinguish members. To support a Vietnam War truce in 1965, middle school student Mary Beth Tinker and her brother, John, wore black anti–Vietnam War armbands that were quickly banned by the school board. [**Fig.13**] The ensuing legal fight culminated with a Supreme Court decision that upheld First Amendment rights for schoolchildren. Mary Beth Tinker continues her work to this day as a free-speech activist focusing on youth issues.

Utilitarian items also function as canvases during marches. Humble buttons and badges have been part of most nineteenth- and twentieth-century protest campaigns. Machine-made, easily worn and distributed, metal pins are the ultimate example of how mass use of a piece of clothing or accessory can create a powerful repeated image. Badges also cleverly convey short slogans that are easy to chant and repeat. The 2016 anti-Trump protests badges read, "When You Elect A Clown, Expect A Circus," and peaceniks in the 1960s wore buttons declaring "Make Love, Not War."

Fig.13 (left)
Mary Beth Tinker and John Tinker, Des Moines, Iowa, December 1965

Fig.14 (right, top)
Original nuclear disarmament symbol design by Gerald Holtom, 1958

Figs.15a–c (right, bottom)
Black-and-white, teal-and-white, and hot-pink-and-black peace buttons, Busy Beaver Button Museum Collection

Figs.16 a, b
Gillian Smith's waistcoat with Miner's
Strike badges, 1980s

The ubiquitous and iconic peace button has traveled the globe on many backpacks and denim jacket lapels, but the logo started as a spark of graphic design inspiration. In 1958, when Gerald Holtom was preparing to join the Aldermaston March for Nuclear Disarmament, the graphic artist began sketching symbols that campaigners could easily draw or stencil onto placards and picket signs. [**Figs.15a–c**]

The original sketch shows his process as he melded two marine semaphores for *N* (nuclear) and *D* (disarmament) together and placed them within a circle. [**Fig.14**] The peace symbol was born and has become, arguably, the most famous protest symbol of the twentieth century.

Carrying on the tradition of buttons and badges as dissent tools, English miners used them to agitate for change as the economy struggled and coal miners were forced out of their jobs by automation in the 1980s. The miners' strike of 1984–85, spurred on by labor unions and raging against mine closures, lasted a year and created drastic fuel shortages and blackouts. Activists throughout England picketed, wearing their everyday work clothes, mining uniforms, and collections of buttons and badges to raise awareness. The Conservative government under Margaret Thatcher won the fight, closing most mines and privatizing the rest. But the material culture remains, as shown in a faded denim biker vest in the Birmingham Museums' collection, owned and worn by strike supporter Gillian Smith. [**Figs.16a, b**] Over time, Smith added layers of badges, buttons, embroidery, and beadwork to the waistcoat, crafting a historical visual document of her experiences.

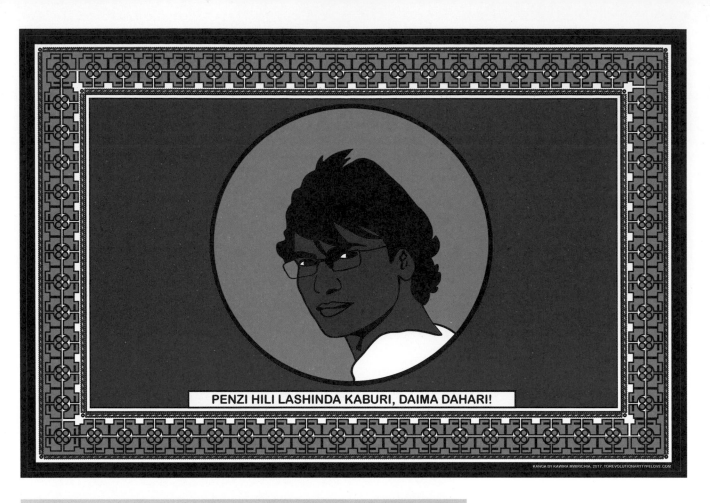

Fig. 17 (above)
Kanga Featuring Bangladeshi activist Xulhaz Mannan by Kawira Mwirichia, 2008

Fig. 18 (left)
"Respect Our Vision" poster, Menominee Warrior Society, 1970s

Fig.19
Dissent necklace by Dissent Pins/
Caitlin Kuhwald, 2019

Wrapping oneself in cloth is one of our earliest human instincts, whether for comfort, shelter, or even communication. In the early years of the American South, messages of freedom were hand stitched onto blankets and quilts, while in Korea, Confucian values and the spirit of common people are patchworked into traditional jogakbo quilts. In 1970s Wisconsin, the Menominee Native Americans agitated for tribal sovereignty. A poignant photograph shows an Indigenous Menominee woman sheathed in an American flag, surrounded by armed soldiers. [**Fig.18**] She is an electrifying visual contrast against the anonymous monotone uniforms of the soldiers. Many Native American tribes (for example, the Chemehuevi and Chumash in California) cherish traditional blankets and shawls for both practical and sentimental reasons, and this Menominee woman fused those meanings with the symbolism of the American flag.

Meanwhile, in modern day Kenya, queer visual artist Kawira Mwirichia reinvents the traditional kanga cloth as an ultramodern symbol for LGBTQ+ rights. Writing for the website Global Voice, journalist Amanda Lichtenstein describes this centuries-old printed textile: "A kanga is the vibrant East African textile featuring Swahili proverbs, [and] is widely known as 'the cloth that speaks.' For centuries, women have exchanged them as gifts, often to communicate messages that would be otherwise taboo."[8] Mwirichia uses her kanga designs to say what she otherwise could not always say in public. This vivid kanga celebrates Bangladeshi gay rights activist Xulhaz Mannan. [**Fig.17**] Written under the image of Mannan is a Bangladeshi proverb, translated into English: "This love overcomes the grave, always and forever!"

And last, but definitely not least, are the Supreme Court collars (or jabots) of Ruth Bader Ginsburg, which she first wore to liven up her black judge's robes and have now come to symbolize social justice for a new generation of young crusaders. Featured in the documentary *RBG* (2018), the collars started as personal fashion statement but have continued as shorthand for Ginsburg's legacy of fighting for and defending gender equality, spawning many easily accessible novelty versions and whimsical Halloween costume homages. A necklace designed by Caitlin Kuhwald for accessory company Dissent Pins turns an ordinary outfit into a moment of microprotest. [**Fig.19**] And while Ginsburg fought for women's rights in her full-length black robes and collar until her death in 2020, some activists do the opposite, as we'll see in the next chapter, and strip off for the cause.

CHAPTER 9

Skin and Symbols: Baring It All

"Clothes, even when omitted, cannot be escaped."

—*Anne Hollander*, Seeing Through Clothes, *1975*

Nakedness can trigger almost any emotion: lust, disgust, shyness, fear, elation, hilarity. Stripped of any exterior protection, nude activists make themselves vulnerable and visible. Walking naked into a public space occupied by those wearing clothing is a simple and elemental method of dissent—the taboos that surround nudity are sure to grab media attention for any given cause. And it is not just nudity that is in play—activists use paint, tattooing, branding and scarification, makeup, piercings, hair styles, and jewelry in addition to nudity to tell stories.

A tribe or culture might typically wear very few clothes but adorn themselves with complex body modifications, paint, and accessories for war and for ceremonies and rituals. Clothing is concerned with covering and concealing the body, and adornment is concerned with decorating and enhancing the body, but both are crucial to the visual identity of humankind. People will endure pain, discomfort, and mutilation to achieve the cultural ideals of beauty in a given era: modern tattoo parlors are full of wincing customers, female (and even male) corsets restrict breathing and movement, and X-rays of the feet of Chinese women who have been subjected to foot-binding show disfigured appendages, folded in half in pursuit of status and tradition.

Notable scholars on the subjects of nudity and dress have devoted entire careers to investigating these complex human behaviors. Groundbreaking anthropologist and dress historian Joanne Bubolz Eicher has delved into how humans adorn and dress themselves and views modesty as a social construct rather than a human instinct. The instinct to adorn our bodies with decoration is in our genes but modesty is usually defined by moral beliefs, cultural forces, governments, and religious leaders. Adornment honors the body; modesty can trigger shame and embarrassment. Protest movements can take advantage of these natural reactions, playing on how we respond to nakedness and morality to grab attention and spur transformation.

Art historian Anne Hollander, author of the seminal book *Seeing Through Clothes* (1975), dissected how the body and clothing are deeply intertwined with our personal image. Throughout the 1970s and 1980s, she studied how art and nudity interplay and in doing so discovered that as fashions change, so do ideal body types. What body parts we show and hide changes wildly according to morality, fashion, religion, sexuality, and geography. The Japanese see the back of the neck as an erogenous zone, worthy of framing in a kimono collar; traditional Muslim cultures often

Fig.1 (opposite)
Monokini by Rudi Gernreich,
2020 Collection

Fig.2 (above)
"Tits" T-shirt by Vivienne Westwood
and Malcolm McLaren, 1975

consider an uncovered head taboo; in France today a woman can lounge at the beach topless, but in the United States she would be arrested.

Fashion disrupter Rudi Gernreich (who parodied the military with his safari suit, as we saw in in Chapter 6) used clothes to reflect the rapidly changing culture of the 1960s and 1970s. The 1964 monokini, a woolen pair of high-waisted swim bottoms with thin straps that skimmed between a woman's breasts, was one of his most outrageous inventions. The Fashion Institute of Design and Merchandising Museum in Los Angeles holds a collection of furious letters written to the maverick designer at the time, including many expressing shock at his "morally corrupt" topless bathing suit. Gernreich never thought the monokini would become popular; that wasn't the point. He purposely used it as a tool to promote sexual freedom. He continued on to design many collections that included lingerie, swimwear, even a see-through underwire bra, but always wove social commentary into his work, believing that fashion would eventually become unisex. A sleek rebranding of his line, complete with high-tech fabrics, reintroduces the monokini to the twenty-first century, so perhaps there is still time for the trend to go viral. [**Fig.1**]

A few years ago, outside of Facebook's New York offices, the controversy about women's breasts and nipples raged on. Artist Spencer Tunick was conducting a large installation of naked people with activist group #WeTheNipple to protest Facebook's censorship of nude art. Naked women were given stickers printed with men's nipples to cover their own, cleverly slipping past censorship laws. The group covered their lower parts with disk-shaped nipple printouts. Even sixty years after the debut of the monokini, the fight for freeing women's breasts is not yet over.

Siouxsie and the Banshees, the 1970s punk/goth superstar band, was one of the few bands that had a female front woman, Susan Ballion. As her alter ego Siouxsie Sioux, Ballion synthesized a pastiche of twentieth-century style cues from old Hollywood glamour to iconic, antiestablishment stage looks. The Tits T-shirt, which sold out at Malcolm McLaren and Vivienne Westwood's SEX boutique, ended up as one of Siouxie's performance costumes. [Fig.2] Clashing the tee with pair of black running shorts, black stockings, short spiked hair, and thick black eyeliner, Siouxsie mashed up anarchist principles with feminist ideals. All the visual clues rejected the stereotypes of how a woman should look and act. Riffing off the idea of the monokini, the Tits T-shirt confronts the viewer with nude breasts, even if they are printed on cotton jersey. It's a clever way of jarring the viewer while subverting the idea of clothing for concealment.

How and why we expose very specific parts of our body can be a way of celebrating cultural struggle. Austrian artist VALIE EXPORT engaged the viewer in a way that made them complicit in her art, showing socially taboo parts of herself in performances to the public. This 1960s art practice was labeled "actionism," a process of interactive public exhibition: EXPORT once encouraged art audiences to feel her breasts through a wooden box positioned on her torso. In a 1969 black-and-white image in the collection of Tate Modern titled *Action Pants: Genital Panic*, EXPORT wears crotchless leather trousers and holds a machine gun, aggressively displaying her genitals. [Fig.3]

Tate Modern frames EXPORT's actions as emblematic of a global cultural shift: "At the end of the 1960s, the notions of guerrilla warfare and revolution on which it played were particularly pertinent—in 1967, the famous Cuban revolutionary Che Guevara was executed, and the following year students rioted in Paris, and the American cities of Baltimore and Washington DC were shaken by civil unrest after the murder of Martin Luther King, Jr."[1] In

Fig.3 (opposite)
Action Pants: Genital Panic by
VALIE EXPORT, 1969

FOTO: PETER HASSMANN

SKIN AND SYMBOLS: BARING IT ALL

Fig.4
Jerry Rubin, Chicago 7 Trial, 1968

creating *Genital Panic*, EXPORT combined two global movements: women's liberation and antiwar activism. EXPORT clashed images of traditionally masculine warfare and guns with intimate feminine body parts, conjuring up a unique piece of protest art.

The 1968 yippie movement (Youth International Party), founded by the colorful revolutionary activist Abbie Hoffman, used humor, performance, costume, and parody to incite change. The Yippies demonstrated for civil rights, held antiwar rallies, and expressed views against social inequality. Their logo, in bright colors and psychedelic 1960s lettering, appeared on helmets, badges, and T-shirts at marches. Hoffman's longtime collaborator Jerry Rubin was escorted from the 1968 House Un-American Activities Committee hearing when he arrived with a semiautomatic rifle; he was bare chested, bearded, and hairy, adorned with necklaces, belts, badges, headbands, and face paint. [Fig.4]

Using satire and comedy (Rubin also dressed as Santa Claus and a Civil War soldier for some of the trials and hearings), Hoffman and Rubin craftily attracted maximum attention while

Fig.5
Ferguson Protests following the police shooting of Michael Brown, Missouri, August 12, 2015

skirting the right side of the law. Because the rules for how one should dress for court were only suggestions, Rubin could attend shirtless and still be allowed in. His naked chest, in black-and-white photographs, contrasted with the suit-and-tie-clad lawyers, the gun-laden court police officers, and the judge's courtroom robe.

In 2015, a young protester demonstrating in Ferguson, Missouri, after the police shooting of Michael Brown covers his face, head, and neck with red fabric to protect against tear gas but simultaneously shows vulnerability by baring his chest. [**Fig.5**] Like Rubin, this man symbolizes so many unnamed protesters using their bodies and their skin to rebel. Unlike Rubin, though, this young man must make daily decisions on how to navigate the world as a Black person. James Baldwin, writing about the Black experience in 1963 articulates, "From my point of view, no label, no slogan, no party, no skin color, and indeed no religion is more important than the human being."[2] Recent Black Lives Matter protests show that more than sixty years after Baldwin wrote those

Fig.6
Artist Pyotr Pavlensky, St. Petersburg,
Russia, May 3, 2013

words, the fight continues for racial equality and safety for Black
individuals. When race can be a matter of life and death, baring
skin can be as potent as covering up.

Using extreme nudity and self-mutilation, Russian contemporary artist Pyotr Pavlensky performs public "actions" similar to
VALIE EXPORT's. Pavlensky once nailed his genitals to the paving
stones on Moscow's Red Square to protest political apathy and
sewed his own lips closed when the rebels from Pussy Riot were
jailed. In an action from 2013 called *Carcass*, Pavlensky encased his
naked body in barbed wire on the steps of the Legislative Assembly
of Saint Petersburg, combining nudity with pain. [**Fig.6**] Pavlensky
won the 2016 Vaclav Havel Prize for Creative Dissent, which, ironically, was withdrawn when Pavlensky declared that his intention
was to donate his prize to an insurgent group.

Photojournalist Glenna Gordon's striking images of women in
far-right movements include a portrait of Erika, an Identity Evropa

member. [Fig.7] Active for the past five years, the organization is dedicated to "preserving white cultural identity."[3] Erika's tattoo of the words "I Will Not Be Silenced" refers to her wish to be independent from the political correctness of modern culture. Appearing almost like a necklace, the tattoo, with its delicate lettering, is placed on her collarbone, giving the tattoo a feminine, ethereal quality. Combined with a hot pink fitted dress, makeup, and short styled hair, the tattoo covertly states her views but from afar reads simply as decoration.

Tattoos have long been entwined with the idea of expressing one's personal identity in most global cultures. A 1907 parlor-card photograph of a young woman wearing pearls, an evening gown, and full sleeves of tattoos echoes the intimacy of Erika's photograph. [Fig.8] The 1891 invention of a mechanical tattoo machine led to the opening of many tattoo parlors, and rumor has it that even Edward, Prince of Wales, got a tattoo in the 1880s. The interplay between clothing, skin, and tattoos allows individuals to share messages if they wish but cleverly permits clothing to cover them up. Thus, a tattoo, branding, piercing, or scarification can be shown or hidden at the wearer's will.

Members of 269 Libération Animale, an Israeli animal rights group, brand themselves as a part of demonstrations and street performances to highlight animal abuse. Founders Zohar Gorelik and Sasha Boojor saw the identification number 269 branded into the skin of a calf rescued from a factory, and the movement was born. Enacting elaborate public scenes during which activists are led from cages in chains and branded with hot irons, 269 members endure physical pain to shock and provoke passersby into experiencing compassion for the suffering of animals. [Fig.9]

Agitators also use writing on skin as a visual tool. The body provides an easy (and cheap!) canvas for messages, slogans, and manifestos. Two images, from one hundred years apart, beautifully highlight how the twentieth century has been framed and defined by women's liberation movements. In the first, from 1915, New Yorker Dorothy Newell stenciled "Votes For Women" across her back and went out in the evening wearing the latest styles. [Fig.10] Backless dresses were all the rage in Western fashion at that time, and women's fashion, art, and society obsessed over seeing a woman dramatically walking away at a ball or opera. Newell covertly used this trend to publicize her agenda. The story was picked up by the *Topeka State Journal* and spread across the nation.

Fig. 7
Erika, American Women of the Far Right
Series by Glenna Gordon, 2017

Fig.8 (above)
Tattooed Lady, Library of Congress
Archives, ca. 1890s

Fig.9 (left)
Branding, 269 Libération Animale, 2012

189

SKIN AND SYMBOLS: BARING IT ALL

A hundred years later in London, SlutWalk members marched in their bras, writing messages and painting their bodies to protest rape culture. Founders Heather Jarvis and Sonya Barnett aim to destigmatize the word "slut" and end slut shaming, welcoming people of all genders, ages, and ethnicities to their marches. In a photograph from the 2012 London Slutwalk march, "A Kiss Is Not A Contract" is written across the back of a young unnamed Black woman with multicolored braids. [Fig.11] As writer bell hooks notes, "Feminist politics can be an integral part of a renewed black liberation struggle."[4]

Paint on skin can transform a face and body. Whether in the context of sports games or used to make tribal markings, pigment, clay, greasepaint, and makeup have been employed by civilizations throughout time to temporarily transform appearances. The painted faces of these men, protesting in Yemen and Tibet respectively, show a common human theme: the deep need to get a message across. [Figs.12, 13] In the city of Sanaa, an antigovernment rebel painted his face in Yemeni flag colors of red, white, and black; in Tibet, activists are covered in paint in the national colors of yellow, blue, white, and red, one of them also wearing mala prayer beads (also known as *threngwa* in Tibetan).

Fig.10 (left)
Activist Dorothy Newell, *Topeka State Chronicle*, November 6, 1915

Fig.11 (right)
Slutwalk march, London, England, September 22, 2012

DRESSING THE RESISTANCE

The first Black man to win the Pulitzer Prize for Journalism, Moneta Sleet Jr. documented hundreds of pivotal twentieth-century moments for *Ebony* magazine. Sleet traveled with Martin Luther King Jr. for more than ten years as King crisscrossed the United States, peacefully protesting for racial equality, and captured two young men at the Selma to Montgomery March in 1965. [Fig.14] The contrast of the white face paint with bold letters spelling *VOTE* across the first man's forehead makes this photograph utterly compelling and unforgettable.

Rosalie Fish, a Cowlitz tribal member in Washington State, ran a track-and-field championship event in 2019 with a shocking red handprint across her face. [Fig.15] Using the stadium as a stage, Fish heightened awareness for Indigenous women, whose deaths and disappearances have not been investigated. With the blessing of her coach and community, Fish ran each race in the honor of a different woman, with the letters *MMIW* (Murdered and Missing Indigenous Women) down her leg. She's proud to be an athlete activist. "There's not really any way that I could separate the two," Fish said. "Being a runner is part of who I am, and caring about these issues is part of who I am."[5]

With dyed orange hair and too many tattoos to count, NBA legend and infamous fashion maverick Dennis Rodman bared it all for the antifur PETA (People for the Ethical Treatment of Animals) ad campaign "Think Ink, Not Mink." [Fig.16] PETA ran the "I'd Rather Go Naked" campaign from 1990 to 2020 to highlight the gruesome impact of farmed fur in the fashion industry. Celebrities across the world stripped down for animal rights. PETA enlisted famous photographers to take the snaps, and with a dose of good humor and irony the ads were unveiled yearly on a billboard towering over Times Square in New York City. As well as tackling animal rights, the campaign celebrated different body shapes and skin tones, championing diversity and individuality.

The animal rights group Anima International stages naked antifur sit-ins during which activists cover their bare bodies in fake blood to highlight animal torture and abuse. [Fig.18] Anima strives to reduce animal suffering, and protesters use their bodies to give voice to animals that cannot speak for themselves. The president of the group, Francisco Vásquez Neira, coordinates large-scale public actions, repeating similar performances year after year across major European cities. Repetition also lends a hand to the cause, whether for artists like VALIE EXPORT and Peter Pavlensky who operate alone, or in group demonstrations, especially in the

Fig.12 (above)
Protester, Sanaa, Yemen, September 29, 2011

Fig.13 (left)
Tibetan Protesters, Dharamsala, India, March 17, 2008

Fig.14
Two Boys, Selma, Alabama, March 1965

absence of clothing or protection. In his book *Fashion Classics* (2003), author Michael Carter reflects on the work of philosopher J. C. Flügel and his theories on nudity and dress: "The reasons we put clothing on are intimately connected to the way we take it off."[6]

Runner Kiran Gandhi was in a dilemma as the 2015 London Marathon approached. She had her period and faced a decision on whether to run the marathon or not, weighing up the chafing that pads might cause, the awkwardness of dealing with tampons on the go, the prospect of canceling an event that she had trained for all year, and the social taboos around women's menstruation. She decided to run with no feminine protection, and photos of Gandhi with blood running down her leggings went viral. [**Fig.17**] In an article for the *Absurdist*, Gandhi wrote about how she had to decide whether to succumb to period-shaming and face the discomfort of tampons and pads while running or be a "liberated boss madame who loved her own body, was running an effing marathon and was not in the mood for being oppressed that day."[7] She chose the latter and ran on behalf of fierce females around the world.

Fig.15 (above)
Rosalie Fish, Cheney, Washington, May 30, 2019

Fig.16 (opposite top left)
Dennis Rodman, "I'd Rather Go Naked" Campaign, PETA, 1990–2020

Fig.17 (opposite top right)
Kiran Gandhi, London Marathon, 2015

Fig.18 (opposite bottom)
Anima Naturalis protesters, Barcelona, December 7, 2015

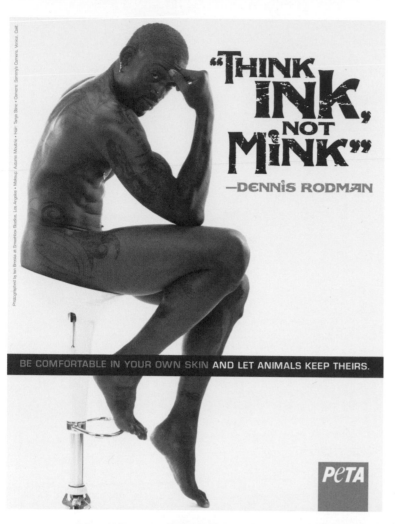

"THINK INK, NOT MINK"

—DENNIS RODMAN

BE COMFORTABLE IN YOUR OWN SKIN **AND LET ANIMALS KEEP THEIRS.**

PeTA

Conclusion

"Nobody is ready for the trailblazers."

—*Cheryl Mills, Hillary Clinton 2016 Presidential Campaign Advisor*

As we look to the future, who will be the new activists? The new punks of the social media world, the new globally connected digital natives? How will they use clothes to celebrate their message? Up-and-coming young activists everywhere are harnessing the power of social media, deftly handling public attention, and using their images and individuality for social change. Clothes, of course, are not their primary focus, but they are a way to set oneself apart in an age permeated by selfies. Remixing and celebrating imagery of past protest movements, new youth movements are creating a postmodern rebel style of their own.

With their six million total Twitter followers, the five young activists profiled below reach young people everywhere, young people speaking thousands of languages and living in almost two hundred countries. Finding a common lingo is pivotal. Nonverbal symbols and short slogans become a crucial ally for these activists in galvanizing a new movement. Photos, graphics, and quotes become ubiquitous through social media and its global reach, and movements can build on the legacy of classic protest garments like the "message tee." When Greta Thunberg wore an "Antifascist All Stars" tee to meet rock band The 1975 for a recording session to promote action on climate change, fans around the world jumped online to buy one of their own. In a 2019 *NME* article, The 1975 lead singer Matty Healy described Thunberg as "the most punk person he's ever met."[1]

Dress historian Carol Tulloch describes the use of fashion and dress to amplify social movements as "style activism." The paintings, photographs, etchings, sculptures, and illustrations we've seen throughout this book document "a moment in life when the styled self is captured in activist activity."[2] Youth movements are redefining how future generations will look, celebrating the clash of dress and protest through hundreds of minute style choices, eclectic and unique. Tulloch notes that style activism isn't only high fashion, although it can be. Ordinary, everyday dress can help frame a new movement as accessible to all. It doesn't have to be expensive—in fact, it's better if it's not, so that engaged social media followers can easily afford to copy a new style activist's look.

A yellow slicker, long brown braids, knitted scarf, and mittens define seventeen-year-old Thunberg's protest style. [Fig.1] As the founder of Fridays for Future, the youngest *Time* Person of the Year, and a Nobel Peace Prize nominee, she has now added message masks to her look with the Fridays for Future organization logo printed boldly in black on white fabric. Knowing that her

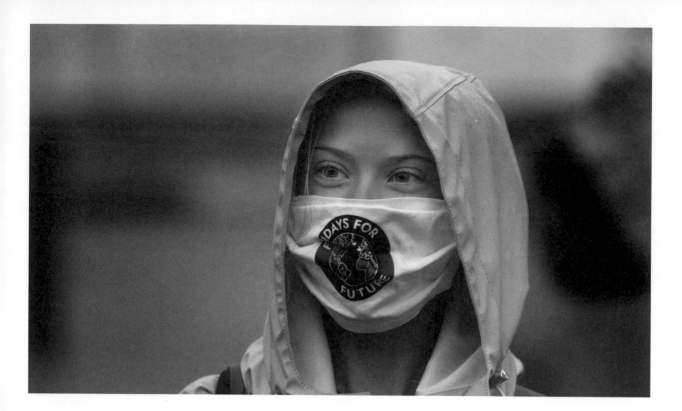

photo will be shown by news outlets around the world, she makes
sure that her clothes are communicating a message: I'm ready for
any weather, and I'm marching until change happens. Thunberg
backs up her iconic silhouette with zero waste wardrobe eth-
ics—she buys primarily secondhand clothes in an effort to offset
fashion waste. She collaborates with climate change organization
Extinction Rebellion, which urges supporters to stamp recycled or
deadstock T-shirts with the organization logo rather than buying
new ones. The "Antifascist All Stars" tee is one of many political
tees in Thunberg's arsenal. Her ethos has now come full circle:
tween activists wear T-shirts emblazoned with Thunberg herself,
her face under her yellow raincoat, wearing fingerless gloves,
secondhand jeans, and Doc Martens.

"You could wear a beret, but when you tilt it to the side, you
go from Parisian to Black Panther."[3] In a 2018 *Teen Vogue* interview with Brianna Wiest, Yara Shahidi explains how clothes can
be political, and politics can be fashionable. Shahidi, twenty years
old and an actress/activist who attends high-profile events wearing
a mix of haute couture, high street fashion, and vintage pieces,
uses her platform to celebrate a spectrum of Black beauty looks.
[**Fig.2**] Rather than passively wearing fashion on the red carpet, she
actively engages in style activism to reframe images of a young
Black woman. In her book *Fashion and Politics* (2019), editor
Djurdja Bartlett celebrates how fashion prompts dialogue and

Fig.2
Yara Shahidi, CFDA Awards, New York,
June 4, 2019

mends divisions: "As a globally dispersed, emotionally charged and highly visual practice in our image-saturated world, fashion may even go some way to repair old and new injustices, at the same time creating a bridge between politics and economics, so providing a platform for today's most urgent social and cultural conversations."[4] Shahidi is one of many Black celebrities who honor Afro hairstyles, underrepresented fashion designers of color, and forgotten Black design heritage, thus making space for those crucial conversations to bloom.

Through her work with Michelle Obama's Let Girls Learn charity and her own Yara's Club organization, Shahidi promotes education for young women and equity for women of color. She joins many prominent Black individuals in using image to deconstruct and then proudly reconstruct an utterly modern representation of Black culture. Fellow entertainer Alicia Keys went makeup free in 2016, defying expectations and conventional beauty standards of what a woman should look like. And Beyoncé educates her social media followers in Black cultural contributions through compelling performances and films.

The 2018 "Apeshit" video featured Beyoncé and Jay-Z in powerful, ornate tableaux throughout the Louvre Museum. Posing on the marble museum steps with dancers of many races, costumed in dancewear coordinated by skin tone, the Carters reclaimed the Louvre for people of color. While paintings featuring primarily

white European upper classes hung on the walls, a diverse cast of performers re-created the paintings live in the space. Meanwhile, Jay-Z and Beyoncé wore a series of tantalizingly stylish designer outfits, all highlighting their success and wealth. As opposed to Black sitters portrayed as servants in paintings, we see Black billionaires living a life of purposeful resistance against outdated stereotypes that reach back hundreds of years. For Beyoncé's 148 million Instagram devotees, a six-minute video like "Apeshit" is a lesson in art history, the Black body, and racial equality—not a simple feat in an era oversaturated with content and media.

Emma González is highly recognizable at rallies and marches with their close-cropped hair, fresh, bare face, and olive-green Che Guevara–style jacket decked out with slogan buttons and pins. [Fig.3] The high school activist and March for Our Lives founder walked the red carpet at the 2018 Time 100 Gala in a strapless yellow ball gown and dark berry lipstick with their iconic hair, tweeting #BaldiesGetTheJobDone. And at the New York City Pride March in 2018, González rocked a completely different look, with body paint, bright red lips, and a burgundy lace bra with rainbow flags tucked in the straps at the back, like wings. A Marjory Stoneman Douglas student, who survived the high school shooting in Parkland, Florida, González pivots away from conventional twentieth-century feminine stereotypes and easily moves between ball gowns and combat boots. They even joined forces with

Fig.3 (above)
Emma González speaks to the media, Florida, February 17, 2018

Fig.4 (opposite)
Fashion designer Sky Cubacub, Rebirth Garments, 2020

Pussyhat Project cofounder Krista Suh, who designed knitted fingerless "evil eye" gloves to support the March for Our Lives. For new youth movements, there is not one style-activism look, there are many.

These twenty-first-century activists are (perhaps unconsciously) referencing monks and ascetics with their gender-neutral look: What better inspiration than Joan of Arc, with her shaved head and gender-neutral appearance? González's pared-down approach to their visual image and no-nonsense rebel attitude gain them more Twitter followers than the National Rifle Association, while their look is reflected back at us on television by actors like Asia Kate Dillon, the first openly nonbinary actor on prime time, playing a revolutionary nonbinary character on HBO's *Billions*. In the current climate of fast fashion, online ordering, and social media posts, videos of González wearing rainbow flags get instant mass distribution—and so does the message.

Disability advocate and self-proclaimed founder of "Queer Crip Dress Reform," Sky Cubacub melds activism, fine metalworking, and cutting-edge fashion in a celebration of queer, trans, and disabled style. [Fig.4] Cubacub founded Rebirth Garments in 2014, when they saw the need for garments that broke gender boundaries. In the studio, Cubacub spends hours crafting custom chainmaille (a centuries-old practice of weaving intricate, interlinked pieces of metal to form a flexible layer of armor) to sell alongside chest binders, vibrant tops, pants, and wearables. Cubacub practices "radical visibility," their brand of inclusivity for all sizes, shapes, and abilities (seen and unseen, physical and mental). In speaking about hand-making chainmaille, they note that "I experience the slow and thoughtful process as calming to my mind…this emotional armor gives me the courage to go out into the world as a multiply marginalized person."[5]

"To me, activism is simple: activism is kindness, respect, and love," says young drag performer Desmond is Amazing. [Fig.5] Desmond Napoles (his real name) shows that the image *is* the message. Using costume, dress, jewelry, and wigs to promote LGBTQ+ rights, Desmond joyously detaches gender from clothing, refashioning himself as an ultramodern style activist. Gender freedom means grabbing inspiration from every corner of dress history: men's heels from the eighteenth-century French royal court, men's pleated skirts from ancient Egypt, men's jewelry and adornment from pan-African tribal costumes. The ideas of femininity, masculinity, and body image that are coursing through society provoke conversation about cultural norms and equality, and thirteen-year-old Desmond is Amazing projects them onto his fashioned body.

Many new-generation rebels use their daily life and simple human interactions to place social change front and center. While mass protests are, of course, critical, so too are daily microprotests. A microprotest can be as simple as being yourself and flouting social norms: the biologically male Hijras, the third gender in India, dress and live as women, sometimes wearing makeup and long hair, and are often discriminated against, left homeless, or living in poverty.

Daily cross-dressing can be a personal, individual protest. This is cross-dressing in the face of danger—people risking punishment and even death for wearing the clothes of a different gender. Cross-dressing may legitimately be performative and associated with comedy and outrageousness, but sometimes it is a performance of simply living. Going through daily life in an authentic way can be a monumental form of resistance for individuals who do not follow the status quo. Cultures are beginning to become more accepting of nonbinary gender identities: Germany passed a draft law in 2018 allowing a third gender choice on official documents, while Thailand, Pakistan, Canada, Denmark, and others have added nonbinary options for citizens.

The five young activists celebrated here encapsulate how hair, makeup, fashion, gender, social media, and celebrity can be fused

Fig.5
LGBTQ+ activist Desmond Napoles,
New York, March 13, 2019

into style activism. The alt-right is leaning into a clean-cut, anonymous, uniform way of dressing and cutting their hair, while progressive activists like Thunberg, González, Shahidi, Cubacub, and Napoles revel in individuality, originality, and creative expression. This polarization reflects a wider trend in societal unrest, as we've seen in previous eras: the clean-cut, aggressive skinhead look versus the freeform, handmade hippie aesthetic.

The Greater Good Science Center, based at University of California, Berkeley, highlighted the idea of polarization in a 2019 article that discusses how "social media...[amps] up moral and emotional messages while organizing people into digital communities based on tribal conflicts."[6] Of course, humanity has been organizing itself into tribes for millennia, but social media does this at hyper speed, enabling society to tweet, retweet, react, meme, and divide digital communities. Perhaps this rapid cycle creates rapid division. Dress, fashion, makeup, hair, and adornment are the windows through which we can envision two possible future scenarios: opposing social tribes pushing further away from each other versus deliberately pulling toward unity. Our choice now is whether we continue to polarize or come back together as a twenty-first-century global community.

Acknowledgments

This book is dedicated to the countless wise and talented mentors who have passed on their knowledge and experience to the up-and-coming generations that followed them. To my mentors, for their patience, guidance, inspiration, and generosity: costume designer and educator Sarah Nash Gates; Aileen Ribeiro, my professor of dress history at the Courtauld Institute; the incomparable Jane Greenwood, my Yale professor of costume design; and in honor of Ming Cho Lee, mentor to thousands of theater designers around the world.

Many organizations, understaffed because of the COVID-19 crisis, nevertheless made special effort to assist with images: the Smithsonian, the Victoria and Albert Museum, the Rokeby Museum, the Museum of Native American History, the Civil War Museum, the National Portrait Gallery London, Kent State Museum, and Denise McIver at the California African American Museum.

Thanks to PETA, CODEPINK, the Yes Men, Anima Naturalis, and 269 Libération Animale for providing photographs of their activists in action.

A number of talented artists, designers, and photographers and their estates contributed images to this book, and I would like to thank each of them: John Ahearn and Rigoberto Torres, Janette Beckman, Ozwald Boateng, Drew Cameron, Dissent Pins and Kaitlin Kuhwald, Glenna Gordon, Georgina Hayman, Osborne Macharia, Madame Gandhi, Katherine McClelland, Kawira Mwirichia, Faith Ringgold, Andrew Shanahan, Masayoshi Sukita, and Miko Underwood.

Thank you to Alex Hatfield and Lily Windsor for assistance in picture research and to John Searle and Jennifer Hudin at the Berkeley Social Ontology Group for encouraging me to write this book after inviting me to speak at a 2016 symposium talk on protest and dress.

Leigh Eisenman, my literary agent at Mackenzie Wolf, inspired me with her patience, cheerfulness, and insight throughout the proposal and publishing process. I'm deeply grateful to Jennifer Thompson at Princeton Architectural Press for supporting this book from the very beginning, and to my editor Kristen Hewitt for her detailed and careful suggestions and wise feedback. And to designer Natalie Snodgrass and the PAP design team, who crafted a bold and elegant layout for the book.

To my husband, Mike Elam, for taking care of our young daughter, Mina, in the middle of the pandemic while I wrote this book and to my parents, Miroslav and Helena Benda, and my brother, Cyril Benda, for their unwavering love. Finally, to my writing partner, a feisty black cat named Giuseppina, who reminded me every day that we must speak for the ones with no voice and agitate for the ones who cannot advocate for themselves.

Notes

INTRODUCTION
1. Shahidha Bari, *Dressed: A Philosophy of Clothes* (New York: Basic Books, 2020), 16.
2. Quentin Bell, "The Incorrigible Habit: A Study of Dress Reform in England," *History Today Magazine* 1, no. 3 (1951).
3. Troy Patterson, "The Common Man's Crown," *New York Times Magazine*, April 1, 2015, www.nytimes.com/2015/04/05 /magazine/the-common-mans-crown.html.
4. Jane Howard, "Doom and Glory of Knowing Who You Are," *Life*, May 24, 1963, 88.

CHAPTER 1
1. Tanisha C. Ford, "SNCC Women, Denim and the Politics of Dress," *Journal of Southern History* 79, no. 3 (August 2013): 625–58.
2. Email interview with fashion designer Miko Underwood, October 26, 2020.
3. Denim Collective website, accessed October 15, 2020, www.oakandacornbrand.com/the-denim-collective.
4. Yinka Shonibare website, accessed October 15, 2020, www.yinkashonibare.com/home/.
5. Ibid.
6. John Gillow and Nicholas Barnard, *Traditional Indian Textiles* (London: Thames & Hudson, 1991), 6.
7. David C. Ward, Dorothy Moss, and John Fagg, *The Sweat of Their Face: Portraying American Workers*, (Washington, DC: Smithsonian Books, 2017), 13.

CHAPTER 2
1. Eric R. Wolf, *Europe and the People Without History* (Berkeley: University of California Press, 1982), 391.
2. James C. Scott, *Weapons of the Weak: Everyday Forms of Peasant Resistance* (New Haven, CT: Yale University Press, 1985), 299.
3. Marlon Brando, *Brando: Songs My Mother Taught Me* (New York: Random House, 1994), 93.
4. George Melly, *Revolt into Style: The Pop Arts in Britain* (Middlesex, England: Penguin Books, 1970), 35.
5. Malcolm X, *The Autobiography of Malcolm X (As Told to Alex Haley)* (New York: Ballantine Books, 1992), chapter 3.
6. Stuart Cosgrove, "The Zoot Suit and Style Warfare," *History Workshop Journal* 18, no. 1 (Autumn 1984): 78.
7. Claire Wilcox, *Vivienne Westwood* (London: V&A Publications, 2004), 15.
8. Allen Ginsberg, "Demonstration or Spectacle as Example, As Communication; or How to Make a March/Spectacle," in *Deliberate Prose: Selected Essays, 1952–1995*, ed. Bill Morgan (New York: Perennial, 2000).
9. Leonee Ormond, "Female Costume in Aesthetic Movement of the 1870 and 1880s," *Costume* 2, no. 1 (1968): 33.
10. Christine Ruane, "Subjects into Citizens: The Politics of Clothing in Imperial Russia," in *Fashioning the Body Politic: Dress, Gender, Citizenship*, ed. Wendy Parkins (Oxford: Berg, 2002), 58.

CHAPTER 3
1. Christopher Breward, *The Culture of Fashion* (Manchester: Manchester University Press, 1995), 132–33.
2. J. C. Flügel, *The Psychology of Clothes* (London: Hogarth Press, 1950), 112.
3. Aileen Ribeiro, *Fashion in the French Revolution* (New York: Holmes & Meier Publishers, 1988), 70.
4. Kimberly Chrisman-Campbell, *Fashion Victims: Dress at the Court of Louis XVI and Marie-Antoinette* (New Haven, CT: Yale University Press, 2015), 287.
5. Quote courtesy of Georgina Hayman, interview with the author, Paris, France, 2020.
6. Roland Barthes, *Oeuvres Completes 1942–1961* (Paris: Seuil, 2002), 1:749.
7. George Melly, *Revolt into Style: The Pop Arts in Britain* (Middlesex, England: Penguin Books, 1970), 35.
8. Sarah Mower, "Katharine Hamnett, London's Activist Fashion Warrior, Is Back With a Sustainable Buy-Now Collection," *Vogue*, September 1, 2017, www.vogue.com/article /katharine-hamnett-launches-sustainable-buy-now-collection.
9. Molly Young, "Muslim Model Halima Aden on Defying Beauty Standards," *Allure*, June 20, 2017, www.allure.com /story/halima-aden-cover-story-july-2017.
10. Tariq Zaidi, "Meet the Sapeuses of Brazzaville," *Al Jazeera*, April 4, 2019, www.aljazeera.com/gallery/2019/3/4 /meet-the-sapeuses-of-brazzaville.
11. Ozwald Boateng, "History," accessed January 22, 2021, www.ozwaldboateng.co.uk/history.
12. Monica L. Miller, *Slaves to Fashion: Black Dandyism and the Styling of Black Diasporic Identity* (Durham, NC: Duke University Press, 2009), 14–15.
13. Email interview with photographer Osborne Macharia, September 21, 2020.

CHAPTER 4
1. Thorstein Veblen, *The Theory of the Leisure Class* (Amherst, NY: Prometheus Books, 1998), 136.
2. Ibid., 167.
3. Anne Hollander, *Sex and Suits* (New York: Alfred A. Knopf, 1994), 98.
4. Telephone interview with Pussyhat Project cofounder Jayna Zweiman, March 8, 2021.
5. Hinda Mandell, ed, *Crafting Dissent* (Lanham, MD: Rowman & Littlefield, 2019), 124.
6. Ibid., 127.
7. Kassia St. Clair, *The Golden Thread: How Fabric Changed History* (New York: Liveright Publishing Corporation, 2018), 2.
8. Jacqueline M. Atkins, *Wearing Propaganda* (New Haven, CT: Yale University Press, December 15, 2005), 21.
9. 511 Tactical website, accessed August 12, 2020, www.511tactical.com/tropi-camo-short-sleeve-shirt.html.
10. Andrew Anglin, accessed 2018, www.dailystormer.su/.
11. National Policy Institute Website, accessed November 2020 (now banned), redirecting to www.alternativeright.com/.

CHAPTER 5
1. Wassily Kandinsky, *Concerning the Spiritual in Art* (New York: Dover Publications, 1977), 23.
2. Kamala Harris, quoted from vice-presidential nomination acceptance speech, Wilmington, Delaware, November 2020.
3. Patrick Symes, *Werner's Nomenclature of Color: Adapted to Zoology, Botany, Chemistry and the Arts* (Washington, DC: Smithsonian Books, 2018).
4. Telephone interview with Pussyhat Project cofounder Jayna Zweiman, March 8, 2021.
5. Victoria Finlay, *Color: A Natural History of the Palette* (New York: Ballantine Books, 2002), 203.
6. Joyce Storey, *Dyes and Fabrics* (London: Thames & Hudson, 1978), 60.

CHAPTER 6
1. Mary Vincent, "Camisas Nuevas: Style and Uniformity in the Falange Espanola, 1933–43," in *Fashioning the Body Politic: Dress, Gender, Citizenship*, ed. Wendy Parkins (Oxford: Berg, 2002), 168.
2. Bill Dunn, *Uniforms* (London: Laurence King Press, 2009), 12.
3. Sol Stern, "The Call of the Black Panthers," *New York Times Magazine*, August 6, 1967, 186.
4. Lidya Zaletova, *Revolutionary Costume* (New York: Rizzoli, 1987), 36.
5. Antonia Finnane, *Changing Clothes in China* (London: Hurst Publishers, 2007), 239.
6. Nina S. Hyde, "Back in Fashion," *Washington Post*, November 22, 1979.
7. Courtesy Drew Cameron, Combat Paper™, interview with the author, 2020.
8. Ibid.

CHAPTER 7
1. Bill Weber and David Weissman, *The Cockettes* (GranDelusion, 2002).
2. Sisters of Perpetual Indulgence website, accessed May 31, 2020, www.thesisters.org/sistory.
3. Cally Blackman, "How The Suffragettes Used Fashion to Further Their Cause," *Guardian*, October 8, 2015, www.theguardian.com/fashion/2015/oct/08/suffragette-style-movement-embraced-fashion-branding.
4. Anne Hollander, *Seeing Through Clothes* (Berkeley: University of California Press, 1975), 239.
5. Stella Bruzzi, *Undressing Cinema: Clothing and Identity in the Movies* (London: Routledge, 1997), 175.
6. Guerrilla Girls website, accessed July 23, 2020, www.guerrillagirls.com/.
7. Daphne Brooks, "100 Years Ago, 'Crazy Blues' Sparked A Revolution for Black Women Fans," *New York Times*, August 10, 2020, www.nytimes.com/2020/08/10/arts/music/mamie-smith-crazy-blues.html.
8. Steeve O. Buckridge, *The Language of Dress: Resistance and Accommodation in Jamaica, 1760–1890* (Kingston, Jamaica: University of the West Indies Press, 2004), 97.
9. Email interview with Yes Men cofounder Mike Bonanno, October 12, 2020.

CHAPTER 8
1. Anne Smart Martin, "Makers, Buyers, and Users: Consumerism as a Material Culture Framework," *Winterthur Journal* 28, no. 2/3 (Summer/Autumn 1993): 141.
2. Donald A. Norman, *Emotional Design* (New York: Basic Books, 2004), 221.
3. Walter Scheidel, "Slavery in the Roman Economy," *Princeton/Stanford Working Papers in Classics*, September 2010, Version 1.0, 4.
4. Photographer Mohammed Zaanoun, email interview with the author, April 3, 2021
5. Djurdja Bartlett, ed., *Fashion and Politics* (New Haven, CT: Yale University Press, 2019), 126.
6. Joanne B. Eicher, ed., *Dress and Ethnicity* (Oxford: Berg, 1999), 225.
7. FIDM Museum & Galleries blog, "The 'It' Bag of 1825," May 22, 2015, blog.fidmmuseum.org/museum/2015/05/the-it-bag-of-18.html.
8. Amanda Lichtenstein, "A Kenyan Artist Designs Revolutionary 'Kanga,' Celebrating Queer Love Around The World," *Global Voice*, August 18, 2017, globalvoices.org/2017/08/18/a-kenyan-artist-designs-revolutionary-kanga-celebrating-queer-love-around-the-world/.

CHAPTER 9
1. Elizabeth Manchester, "Action Pants: Genital Panic 1969," *Tate Modern Art & Artists*, March 2007, www.tate.org.uk/art/artworks/export-action-pants-genital-panic-p79233.
2. Raoul Peck, *I Am Not Your Negro* (Magnolia Pictures, 2016).
3. Identity Evropa website, accessed July 27, 2020, www.identityevropa.com/.
4. bell hooks, *Black Looks: Race and Representation* (New York: Routledge, 2014), 42.
5. Megan Rowe, "Leaving Her Mark: Native High Schooler Uses State Track Meet to Raise Awareness for Missing and Murdered Women," *Spokesman Review*, May 20, 2019, www.spokesman.com/stories/2019/may/30/leaving-her-mark-native-high-schooler-uses-state-t/.
6. Michael Carter, "J. C. Flugel and the Nude Future," in *Fashion Classics: From Carlyle to Barthes* (Oxford: Berg, 2003), 116.
7. Kiran Gandhi, "Here's Why I Ran the London Marathon on the First Day of My Period—and Chose Not to Wear a Tampon," *Independent*, August 14, 2015, www.independent.co.uk/voices/comment/here-s-why-i-ran-london-marathon-first-day-my-period-and-chose-not-wear-tampon-10455176.html.

CONCLUSION
1. Andrew Trendell, "The 1975's Matty Healy on 'Iconic' Greta Thunberg: 'She's the Most Punk Person I've Ever Met,'" *NME*, September 25, 2019, www.nme.com/news/music/1975s-matty-healy-greta-thunberg-punk-person-ive-ever-met-2551245.
2. Djurdja Bartlett, ed., *Fashion and Politics* (New Haven, CT: Yale University Press, 2019), 91.
3. Brianna Wiest, "Yara Shahidi Explains Why Fashion Can Be A Political Statement," *Teen Vogue*, February 24, 2018, www.teenvogue.com/story/yara-shahidi-explains-fashion-political-statement.
4. Bartlett, *Fashion and Politics*, 13.
5. Sky Cubacub, as quoted from interview with the author by email, January 25, 2021.
6. Zaid Jilani and Jeremy Adam Smith, "What is the True Cost of Polarization in America?" *Greater Good Magazine*, March 4, 2019, www.greatergood.berkeley.edu/article/item/what_is_the_true_cost_of_polarization_in_america.

Bibliography

DRESS HISTORY AND THEORY

Barber, Elizabeth Wayland. *Women's Work: The First 20,000 Years*. New York: W. W. Norton, 1994.

Barnes, Ruth, and Joanne B. Eicher. *Dress and Gender: Making and Meaning*. Oxford: Berg, 1992.

Boucher, Francois. *A History of Costume in the West*. London: Thames & Hudson, 1996.

Chrisman-Campbell, Kimberly. *Fashion Victims: Dress at the Court of Louis XVI and Marie-Antoinette*. New Haven, CT: Yale University Press, 2015.

Cumming, Valerie. *The Visual History of Costume Accessories*. London: B. T. Batsford, 1998.

Damase, Jacques. *Sonia Delaunay: Fashion and Fabrics*. London: Thames & Hudson, 1991.

Davenport, Milia. *The Book of Costume*. New York: Crown Publishers, 1948.

Dunn, Bill. *Uniforms*. London: Laurence King Publishing, 2009.

Eicher, Joanne B. *Dress and Ethnicity*. Oxford: Berg, 1999.

Eicher, Joanne B., Sandra Lee Evenson, and Hazel A. Lutz. *The Visible Self: Global Perspectives on Dress, Culture, and Society*. New York: Fairchild Publications, 2008.

Finnane, Antonia. *Changing Clothes in China*. London: Hurst Publishers, 2007.

Fussell, Paul. *Uniforms: Why We Are What We Wear*. Boston: Houghton Mifflin Company, 2002.

Geczy, Adam. *Fashion and Orientalism: Dress, Textiles and Culture from the 17th to the 21st Century*. London: Bloomsbury Academic Publishing, 2015.

Griggs, Claudine. *S/HE: Changing Sex and Changing Clothes*. Oxford: Berg, 1998.

Hollander, Anne. *Sex and Suits*. New York: Alfred A. Knopf, 1994.

---. *Seeing Through Clothes*. Berkeley: University of California Press, 1973.

Hope, Thomas. *Costumes of the Greeks and Romans*. New York: Dover Publications, 1962.

Houston, Mary G. *Medieval Costume in England and France: The 13th, 14th, and 15th Centuries*. New York: Dover Publications, 1939.

Lansdell, Avril. *Occupational Costume 1776–1976*. Shire Album 27.

Laver, James. *Modesty in Dress*. Crawley, England: William Heinemann, 1969.

Lurie, Allison. *The Language of Clothes*. New York: Random House, 1983.

Parkins, Wendy, ed. *Fashioning the Body Politic: Dress, Gender, Citizenship*. Oxford: Berg, 2002.

Pointon, Marcia. *Hanging the Head: Portraiture and Social Formation in Eighteenth-Century England*. New Haven, CT: Yale University Press, 1993.

Scott, A. C. *Chinese Costume in Transition*. Kuala Lumpur: Donald Moore, 1958.

Shukla, Pravina. *Costume: Performing Identities through Dress*. Bloomington: Indiana University Press, 2015.

Styles, John. *The Dress of the People: Everyday Fashion in 18th Century England*. New Haven, CT: Yale University Press, 2007.

Ribeiro, Aileen. *Fashion in the French Revolution*. New York: Holmes & Meier Publishers, 1988.

---. *The Gallery of Fashion*. Princeton, NJ: Princeton University Press, 2000.

Ribeiro, Aileen, and Valerie Cummings. *A Visual History of Costume*. London: B. T. Batsford, 1989.

Roach, Mary Ellen, and Joanne Bubolz Eicher, eds. *Dress, Adornment and the Social Order*. New York: John Wiley & Sons, 1965.

---. *Dress and Identity*. Oxford: Berg, 1992.

St. Clair, Kassia. *The Golden Thread: How Fabric Changed History*. New York: Livewright Publishing Corporation, 2018.

Suthrell, Charlotte. *Unzipping Gender: Sex, Cross-Dressing, and Culture*. Oxford: Berg, 2004.

Tortora, Phyllis G. *Dress, Fashion and Technology: From Prehistory to the Present*. London: Bloomsbury Academic Publishing, 2015.

Waterfield, Giles, and Anne French. *Below Stairs: 400 Years of Servants' Portraits*. London: National Portrait Gallery Publications, 2003.

FASHION

Bolton, Andrew. *Bravehearts: Men In Skirts*. London: V&A Publications, 2003.

Breward, Christopher. *The Culture of Fashion*. Manchester: Manchester University Press, 1995.

Brown, Sass. *Eco Fashion*. London: Laurence King Publishing, 2010.

Kanai, Jun I. *Japonism in Fashion*. Tokyo: Kyoto Costume Institute, 1996.

Khabeer, Su'ad Abdul. *Muslim Cool: Race, Religion, and Hip Hop in the United States*. New York: New York University Press, 2016.

Kirkham, Pat, ed. *Women Designers in the USA, 1900–2000*. New York: Yale University Press, 2001.

Klanten, Robert. *Africa Rising*. Berlin: Die Gestalten Verlag, 2016.

Lewis, Reina. *Muslim Fashion: Contemporary Style Cultures*. Durham, NC: Duke University Press, 2015.

Mauriès, Patrick. *Androgyne: Fashion + Gender*. New York: Thames & Hudson, 2017.

Newman, Cathy. *Fashion*. Washington, DC: National Geographic Society, 2001.

Paulicelli, Eugenia. *Fashion Under Fascism: Beyond the Black Shirt*. Oxford: Berg, 2004.

Root, Regina A. *The Latin American Fashion Reader*. Oxford: Berg, 2005.

Steele, Valerie. *Fetish: Fashion, Sex and Power*. Oxford: Oxford University Press, 1996.

---. *Pink: The History of a Punk, Pretty, Powerful Color*. New York: Thames & Hudson, 2018.

---. *A Queer History of Fashion: From the Closet to the Catwalk*. New Haven, CT: Yale University Press, 2013.

Welters, Linda, and Abby Lillethun. *Fashion History: A Global View*. London: Bloomsbury Visual Arts, 2018.

Wilcox, Claire. *Radical Fashion*. London: V&A Publications, 2001.

---. *Vivienne Westwood*. London: V&A Publications, 2004.

PHILOSOPHY OF DRESS AND FASHION

Bari, Shahidha. *Dressed: A Philosophy of Clothes*. New York: Basic Books, 2020.

Barthes, Roland. *The Fashion System*. Translated by Matthew Ward and Richard Howard. Berkeley: University of California Press, 1990.

Bell, Quentin. *On Human Finery*. London: Allison & Busby, 1992.

Carter, Michael. *Fashion Classics: From Carlyle to Barthes*. Oxford: Berg, 2003.

Johnson, Donald Clay, and Helen Bradley Foster. *Dress Sense: Emotion and Sensory Experiences of the Body and Clothes*. Oxford: Berg, 2007.

Searle, John R. *The Construction of Social Reality*. New York: Free Press, 1995.

---. *Mind, Language and Society: Philosophy in the Real World*. New York: Basic Books, 1998.

Simmel, Georg. "Fashion." *American Journal of Sociology* 62, no. 6 (May 1957): 541–58.

Veblen, Thorstein. *The Theory of the Leisure Class*. Amherst, NY: Prometheus Books, 1899/1998.

MENSWEAR

Blackman, Cally. *One Hundred Years of Menswear*. London: Laurence King Publishing, 2009.

Chenoune, Farid. *A History of Menswear*. Paris: Flammarion, 1993.

De Marly, Diana. *Fashion for Men: An Illustrated History*. New York: Holmes & Meier Publishers, 1985.

Flusser, Alan. *Dressing the Man*. New York: Harper Collins Publishers, 2002.

Gunn, Douglas, Roy Luckett, and Josh Sims. *Vintage Menswear: A Collection from the Vintage Showroom*. London: Laurence King Publishing, 2012.

Schoeffler, O. E., and William Gale. *Esquire's Encyclopedia of 20th Century Menswear*. New York: McGraw-Hill Book Company, 1973.

Sims, Josh. *Icons of Men's Style*. London: Laurence King Publishing, 2011.

SUBCULTURE STYLE

Alvarez, Luis. *The Power of the Zoot: Youth Culture and Resistance During World War II*. Berkeley: University of California Press, 2008.

Aoki, Shoichi. *FRUiTS*. New York: Phaidon, 2001.

Beckman, Janette. *Made in the UK: The Music of Attitude 1977–1983*. Brooklyn, NY: powerHouse Books, 2007.

Begum, Lipi, Rohit K. Dasgupta, and Reina Lewis. *Styling South Asian Youth Cultures: Fashion, Media & Society*. London: Tauris, 2018.

Bolton, Andrew, Richard Hell, John Lydon, and Jon Savage. *Punk: Chaos to Couture*. New Haven, CT: Yale University Press, 2013.

De La Haye, Amy, and Cathie Dingwall. *Surfers, Soulies, Skinheads, & Skaters: Subcultural Style from the Forties to the Nineties*. Woodstock, NY: Overlook Press, 1996.

Gorman, Paul, Keanan Duffty, and B. P. Fallon. *Rebel Rebel: Anti-Style*. New York: Universe Publishing, 2009.

Greer, Fergus. *Leigh Bowery Looks*. London: Violette Editions, 2002.

Hebdige, Dick. *Subculture: The Meaning of Style*. New York: Methuen & Co., 1987.

McClendon, Alphonso D. *Fashion and Jazz: Dress, Identity and Subcultural Improvisation*. London: Bloomsbury Academic Publishing, 2015.

Melly, George. *Revolt into Style: The Pop Arts in Britain*. Harmondsworth, England: Penguin Books, 1970.

Peiss, Kathy. *Zoot Suit: The Enigmatic Career of an Extreme Style*. Philadelphia: University of Pennsylvania Press, 2011.

Sklar, Monica. *Punk Style*. London: Bloomsbury Academic Publishing, 2013.

Wortmann Weltge, Sigrid. *Bauhaus Textiles: Women Artists and the Weaving Workshop*. New York: Thames & Hudson, 1993.

Zaletova, Lidya, Fabio Ciofi degli Atti, and Franco Panzini. *Revolutionary Costume: Soviet Clothing and Textiles of the 1920s*. New York: Rizzoli Publications, 1989.

BLACK STYLE

Bingham, Howard L. *Howard L. Bingham's Black Panthers 1968*. Pasadena, CA: AMMO Books, 2009.

Buckridge, Steeve O. *The Language of Dress: Resistance and Accommodation in Jamaica, 1760–1890*. Kingston, Jamaica: University of the West Indies Press, 2004.

Foster, Helen Bradley. *"New Raiments of Self" African American Clothing in the Antebellum South*. Oxford: Berg, 1997.

Gerzina, Gretchen Holbrook. *Black Victorians/Black Victoriana*. New Brunswick, NJ: Rutgers University Press, 2003.

---. *Black London: Life before Emancipation*. New Brunswick, NJ: Rutgers University Press, 1995.

Huggins, Nathan Irvin. *Harlem Renaissance*. Oxford: Oxford University Press, 1971.

McCollom, Michael. *The Way We Wore: Black Style Then*. New York: Glitterati, 2014.

Miller, Monica. *Black Dandyism and the Styling of Black Diasporic Identity*. Durham: Duke University Press, 2009.

Reed Miller, Rosemary E. *Threads of Time: The Fabric of History: Profiles of African American Dressmakers and Designers, 1850–2002*. Washington, DC: T&S Press, 2002.

Scott, Georgia. *Headwraps: A Global Journey*. New York: Public Affairs, 2003.

Tulloch, Carol. *The Birth of Cool: Style Narratives of the African Diaspora*. London: Bloomsbury Academic Publishing, 2016.

--- *Black Style*. London: V&A Publishing, 2004.

White, Shane, and Graham White. *Stylin': African American Expressive Culture: From Its Beginnings to the Zoot Suit*. New York: Cornell University Press, 1998.

COSTUME IN FILM

Engelmeier, Regine, and Peter W. Engelmeier, eds. *Fashion in Film*. Munich: Prestel, 1997.

Hollander, Anne. *Moving Pictures*. Cambridge, MA: Harvard University Press, 1991.

Leese, Elizabeth. *Costume Design in the Movies*. New York: Dover Publications, 1991.

Munich, Adrienne. *Fashion in Film*. Bloomington: Indiana University Press, 2011.

Nadoolman Landis, Deborah. *Dressed: A Century of Hollywood Costume Design*. New York: Collins, 2007.

Nadoolman Landis, Deborah, ed. *Hollywood Costume*. London: V&A Publishing, 2012.

Nourmand, Tony, and Graham Marsh. *Hollywood and the Ivy Look*. London: Reel Art Press, 2011.

Rabinowitz, Jonathan, ed. *Hollywood and History: Costume Design in Film*. New York: Thames & Hudson, 1987.

Street, Sarah. *Costume and Cinema: Dress Codes in Popular Film*. London: Wallflower, 2001.

TEXTILES, RESISTANCE, AND CRAFTIVISM

Artists Circle Alliance. *Threads of Resistance*. Artists Circle Alliance, 2013.

Atkins, Jacqueline M., ed. *Wearing Propaganda: Textiles on the Home Front in Japan, Britain, and the United States, 1931–1945*. New Haven, CT: Yale University Press, 2005.

Bendadi, Samira, and Mashid Mohadjerin. *Textile as Resistance*. Antwerp: Hannibal Publishing, 2019.

Bryan-Wilson, Julia. *Fray: Art and Textile Politics*. Chicago: University of Chicago Press, 2017.

Decker, Juilee, and Hinda Mandell, eds. *Crafting Democracy: Fiber Arts and Activism*. Rochester, NY: RIT Press, 2019.

Mandell, Hinda, ed. *Crafting Dissent*. Lanham, MD: Rowman & Littlefield, 2019.

Shaw, Madelyn, and Lynne Zacek Bassett. *Homefront & Battlefield: Quilts & Context in the Civil War*. Lowell, MA: American Textile History Museum, 2012.

MATERIAL CULTURE

Herzog, Lena, and Werner Herzog. *Pilgrims: Becoming the Path Itself*. London: Arcperiplus Publishing Ltd., 2002.

Kalman, Maira. *My Favorite Things*. New York: Harper Design, 2014.

Kreamer, Christine Mullen, and Sarah Fee, eds. *Objects as Envoys: Cloth, Imagery and Diplomacy in Madagascar*. Seattle: Marquand Books, 2002.

Miller, Daniel. *Material Culture and Mass Consumption*. Oxford: Basil Blackwell, 1987.

Parker, Rozsika. *The Subversive Stitch: Embroidery and the Making of the Feminine*. London: I.B. Tauris & Co., Ltd., 2010.

Spivack, Emily. *Worn Stories*. New York: Princeton Architectural Press, 2014.

Zucotti, Paula. *Every Thing We Touch: A 24-Hour Inventory of Our Lives*. London: Penguin Random House, 2015.

PROTEST

Deutsch, Andre. *Protest!: Sixty-Five Years of Rebellion in Photographs*. London: Carlton Publishing Group, 2011.

Glaser, Milton, and Mirko Ilić. *The Design of Dissent*. Beverly, MA: Quarto Publishing Group USA, 2005.

McQuiston, Liz. *Suffragettes to She-Devils*. Hong Kong: Phaidon Press, 1997.

---. *Visual Impact: Creative Dissent in the 21st Century*. New York: Phaidon Press Limited, 2015.

Rogger, Basil, Jonas Vögeli, Ruedi Widmer, and Museum fur Gestaltung Zurich. *Protest: The Aesthetics of Resistance*. Zurich: Lars Muller Publishers, 2018.

Siegler, Bonnie. *Signs of Resistance: A Visual History of Protest in America*. New York: Artisan, 2018.

Young, Ralph. *Make Art Not War: Political Protest Posters from the Twentieth Century*. New York: New York University Press, 2016.

ART

Bindman, David, and Henry Louis Gates Jr., eds. *The Image of the Black in Western Art*. Cambridge, MA: Harvard University Press, 2010.

Farrington, Lisa E. *Creating Their Own Image: The History of African-American Women Artists*. Oxford: Oxford University Press, 2005.

Godfrey, Mark, and Zoé Whitley, eds. *Soul of a Nation: Art in the Age of Black Power*. New York: Distributed Art Publishers, 2017.

Gosling, Lucinda, Hilary Robinson, and Amy Tobin. *The Art of Feminism: Images that Shaped the Fight for Equality, 1857–2017*. London: Chronicle Books, 2018.

Hirsch, Melissa. *Art as Activist: Revolutionary Posters from Central and Eastern Europe*. Washington, DC: Smithsonian Institute Traveling Exhibition Service; New York: Universe Publishing, 1992.

Lampert, Nicolas. *A People's Art History of the United States*. New York: New Press, 2013.

McElroy, Guy C. *Facing History: The Black Image in American Art 1710–1940*. Washington, DC: Bedford Arts, 1990.

Stern, Radu. *Against Fashion: Clothing as Art, 1850–1930*. Cambridge, MA: MIT Press, 1992.

Ward, David C., and Dorothy Moss. *The Sweat of Their Face: Portraying American Workers*. Washington, DC: Smithsonian Books, 2017.

COLOR THEORY

Faiers, Jonathan, and Mary Westerman Bulgarella. *Colors in Fashion*. Oxford: Bloomsbury Visual Arts, 2017.

Finlay, Victoria. *Color: A Natural History of the Palette*. New York: Ballantine Books, 2002.

Gage, John. *Colour and Meaning: Art, Science and Symbolism*. London: Thames & Hudson, 1999.

Guineau, Bernard, and François Delamare. *Colour: Making and Using Dyes and Pigments*. London: Thames & Hudson New Horizons, 1999.

Kandinsky, Wassily. *Concerning the Spiritual in Art*. New York: Dover Publications, 1977.

Loske, Alexandra. *Color: A Visual History from Newton to Modern Color Matching Guides*. Washington, DC: Smithsonian Books, 2019.

St. Clair, Kassia. *The Secret Lives of Color*. New York: Penguin Books, 2016.

Storey, Joyce. *Dyes and Fabrics*. London: Thames & Hudson, 1978.

Symes, Patrick. *Werner's Nomenclature of Color: Adapted to Zoology, Botany, Chemistry and the Arts*. Washington, DC: Smithsonian Books, 2018.

Image Credits

Introduction / Fig. 1: AP Photo/Nick Ut; Fig. 2: Photograph: Jim Watson/AFP via Getty Images, September 04, 2018; Fig. 3: AP Photo/Butch Dill

Chapter 1 / Fig. 1: Memorial Art Gallery, University of Rochester, Marion Stratton Gould Fund, by exchange, and with the support of attendees on the 2019 Frieze Los Angeles art trip. *The Gardener* (Melissa with Bob Marley Shirt) by John Ahearn and Rigoberto Torres, 1997/2007; Fig. 2: © Danny Lyon/Magnum Photos, 1962–64; Fig. 3: Oak & Acorn 2020 Collection/Miko Underwood. Photographer: Peter Osborne, 2020; Fig. 4: Designer: Tomato Košir, Slovenia, 2000; Fig. 5: Courtesy of the FIDM Museum at the Fashion Institute of Design & Merchandising, Los Angeles, California. Gift of Dorothy Washington Sorensen, Photograph: FIDM Museum & Library, Inc.; Fig. 6: Jim West/Alamy Live News; Fig. 7: Caitlin Ochs/Reuters; Fig. 8: Photograph: Iryna Stelmakh, RFE/RL's Ukrainian Service, February 20, 2014; Fig. 9: National Archives, Online Public Access, General Services Administration. National Archives and Records Service; Fig. 10: *Gilets Jaunes Vieux Nice Revendication sur Gilet*. Photograph: Aeroceanaute, Creative Commons Attribution-Share Alike 4.0 International; Fig. 11: Cindy Sherman, Scale Relationship Series, *The Giant*, Guggenheim Museum, 97.4572; Fig. 12: *Nelson Mandela* by Robert McCurdy, 2009. Oil on canvas. National Portrait Gallery, Smithsonian Institution; gift of Ian M. and Annette P. Cumming, The Cumming Collection. © Robert McCurdy; Fig. 13: Asociación Madres Del Plaza De Mayo, Museo De Bicentenario, 2011. Creative Commons Attribution-Share Alike 3.0; Fig. 14: Ghost Dance Shirt, Museum of Native American Heritage, c. 1890–1900. Photograph: Matt Rowe; Fig. 15: *Tamil Nadu Farmers Wear Saree During Protests In Jantar Mantar*, New Delhi, India, April 14, 2017. Photograph: Ravi Choudhary/*Hindustan Times* via Getty Images; Fig. 16: John Singleton Copley, American, 1738–1815, *Paul Revere*, 1768, 30.781. Oil on canvas, 89.22 x 72.39 cm (35 1/8 x 28 1/2 in.), Museum of Fine Arts, Boston. Gift of Joseph W. Revere, William B. Revere and Edward H. R. Revere; Fig. 17: Courtesy of Rokeby Museum, Ferrisburgh, Vermont; Fig. 18: Sojourner Truth Abstract/medium: one photographic print on carte de visite mount: albumen; 10 x 6 cm. Library of Congress; Fig. 19: Soviet Invasion of Czechoslovakia. Public Domain, Central Intelligence Agency, 1968

Chapter 2 / Fig. 1: *The Wild One*, aka: Der Wilde, U.S.A. 1953. Director: Laslo Benedek, featuring: Marlon Brando. United Archives GmbH / Alamy Stock Photo; Fig. 2: Trinity Mirror / Mirrorpix / Alamy Stock Photo; Fig. 3: Everett Collection Historical / Alamy Stock Photo; Fig. 4: mccool / Alamy Stock Photo; Fig. 5: Photograph: Bill Ray/The LIFE Picture Collection via Getty Images; Fig. 6: Photograph: Janette Beckman, courtesy of the photographer; Fig. 7: Photograph: David Dagley/Shutterstock, 1976; Fig. 8: Photograph: Dick Thomas Johnson, Creative Commons 2.0; Fig. 9: Photograph: Terence Spencer/The LIFE Picture Collection via Getty Images; Fig. 10: Courtesy: CSU Archives / Everett Collection, April 8, 1967; Fig. 11: Lebrecht Music & Arts / Alamy Stock Photo; Fig. 12: Library of Congress, LC-DIG-pga-03142; Fig. 13: Evening dress of pleated silk with string of glass beads, designed by Fortuny, Venice, ca. 1920. Given by Mrs. Hollond, Victoria & Albert Museum, London; Fig. 14: Smith Archive / Alamy Stock Photo; Fig. 15: Creative Commons CC0 License; Fig. 16: State Russian Museum Reproduction, SPUTNIK / Alamy Stock Photo; Fig. 17: *Augustus John* by Charles F. Slade, snapshot print enlargement, September 1909. © reserved, collection National Portrait Gallery, London; Fig. 18: Photograph: Hubert Boesl/dpa

Chapter 3 / Fig. 1: Creative Commons CC0 License; Fig. 2: © RMN-Grand Palais / Art Resource, NY. *Louis XVI, King of France and Navarre* (1754–1793), Dressed in Royal Garb in 1779. Oil on canvas. 278 x 198 cm. Inv. MV3890. Photograph: Jean-Marc Manaï; Fig. 3: © RMN-Grand Palais / Art Resource, NY. *Portrait of Marie Antoinette, Queen of France* (1755–1793), ca. 1785. Oil on canvas, 276 x 193 cm. Inv. MV4519. Photograph: Gérard Blot; Fig. 4: © RMN-Grand Palais / Art Resource, NY. *Habit de citoyen de Français* [Costume for a French citizen]. Costume project for a civic costume, 1793. Pen and ink, wash, watercolor, 30 x 20 cm. MV5291; INVDessins830; RF1922; Fig. 5: Purchased with funds provided by Suzanne A. Saperstein and Michael and Ellen Michelson, with additional funding from the Costume Council, the Edgerton Foundation, Gail and Gerald Oppenheimer, Maureen H. Shapiro, Grace Tsao, and Lenore and Richard Wayne (M.2007.211.1078). Los Angeles County Museum of Art; Fig. 6: Creative Commons License CC0; Fig. 7: Lifestyle pictures / Alamy Stock Photo; Fig. 8: François Gérard, *Napoléon Bonaparte Premier Consul, Château de Chantilly*. The Artchives / Alamy Stock Photo; Fig. 9: Photograph: Cecil Beaton. Victoria & Albert Museum, London; Fig. 10: Odette Fabius, courtesy of Georgina Hayman, c. 1942; Fig. 11: Courtesy of the FIDM Museum at the Fashion Institute of Design & Merchandising,

Los Angeles, California. Photograph: Brian Sanderson; Fig. 12: *Chicago Daily Tribune*, courtesy of House of Christian Dior, Paris, France; Fig. 13: © The Metropolitan Museum of Art. Image source: Art Resource, New York. Ensemble. American, 1944. Black cotton and rayon plain weave. The Metropolitan Museum of Art, Gift of Claire McCardell, 1949 (C.I.49.37.30a-d); Fig. 14: Everett Collection Historical / Alamy Stock Photo, 1967; Fig. 15: PA/PA Archive/PA Images; Fig. 16: Photograph by Xavier Collin/Image Press Agency; Fig. 17: Courtesy of Oswald Boateng, Spring/Summer 2020 Collection. Photograph: Jamie Morgan, Model: Dennis Okwera; Fig. 18: Remember The Rude Boy_02, courtesy of photographer Osborne Macharia/K.63 Studio, 2017

Chapter 4 / Fig. 1: © 2020 Faith Ringgold / Artists Rights Society (ARS), New York, Courtesy ACA Galleries, New York; Fig. 2: Keystone Press / Alamy Stock Photo; Fig. 3: Everett Collection Historical / Alamy Stock Photo; Fig. 4: Photograph: Michael Ochs Archives/Getty Images; Fig. 5: Photograph: Jeffrey Mayer. Pictorial Press Ltd / Alamy Stock Photo; Fig. 6: Montgomery, Alabama, United States, 1965; printed 1995. Silver and photographic gelatin on photographic paper. Collection of the Smithsonian National Museum of African American History and Culture, Gift of Tracy Martin and Michelle Martin Lunceford in memory of their father, Spider Martin, ©1965 Spider Martin; Fig. 7: Eve Arnold/Magnum Photos; Fig. 8: Creative Commons, Public Domain; Fig. 9: Keystone Press / Alamy Stock Photo; Fig. 10: Photograph: Douglas Miller/Getty Images; Fig. 11: Topi hat, courtesy of the Kent State Museum Collection, GO Pauline E. Koller, IMO Dr. Marvin R. Koller. Date unknown. Gandhi cap of white khadi cotton fabric, tip, and band in long leaf shape, 5 1/2 in. band folded up to 2 3/4 in.; Fig. 12: Men's Confederate shirt, worn by Edwin Gilliam Booth, Jr, 1863. Courtesy the American Civil War Museum, Richmond, Virginia; Fig. 13: FIDM Museum Purchase, courtesy of the FIDM Museum at the Fashion Institute of Design & Merchandising, Los Angeles, California. Photograph: Brian Sanderson; Fig. 14: Girl's Kimono (*Haregi*), ca. 1940–41 Japan. Rayon (*jinken*); plain weave, printed (silk screen), applied gold paste, 78.7 x 78.7 cm (31 x 31 in.) Gift of Erik Jacobsen, 2015.84.10, Fine Arts Museums of San Francisco; Fig. 15: Photograph: Anthony Crider, Creative Commons Attribution 2.0 Generic License; Fig. 16: Reuters/Jim Bourg; Fig. 17: Pictorial Press Ltd / Alamy Stock Photo; Figs. 18–22: Copyright Gwyn Conaway

Chapter 5 / Fig. 1: Photograph: Mandel Ngan / AFP via Getty Images; Fig. 2: Reuters/Philimon Bulawayo; Fig. 3: Joerg Boethling / Alamy Stock Photo; Fig. 4: Reuters / Alamy Stock Photo; Fig. 5: SOPA Images Limited / Alamy Stock Photo; Fig. 6: AP Photo/Ben Curtis; Fig. 7: Photo by Paula Bronstein/Getty Images; Fig. 8: Reuters/Edgard Garrido/Alamy Stock Photo; Fig. 9: Reuters/Bryn Lennon; Fig. 10: Reuters/Kacper Pempel

Chapter 6 / Fig. 1: Reuters/Stephen Yang/Alamy Stock Photo; Fig. 2: Photograph: Osvaldo Salas. Salas Archive Photos / Alamy Stock Photo; Fig. 3: Reuters/Gleb Garanich; Fig. 4: Photograph: Jack Manning/New York Times Co./Getty Images; Fig. 5: Unidentified Artist, Huey Percy Newton, photolithographic halftone poster. National Portrait Gallery, Smithsonian Institution, c. 1968, Creative Commons CC0; Fig. 6: Cesar Chavez's union jacket, 1993. Donated by Helen F. Chavez, National Museum of American History, Creative Commons CC0; Fig. 7: Everett Collection Historical / Alamy Stock Photo; Fig. 8: David Lagerlof/TT News Agency/ PA Images; Fig. 9: Designs for Leon Trotsky's Red Guard Uniforms, 1918, Creative Commons License 0.0; Fig. 10: Creative Commons License 0.0; Fig. 11: Constance Markievicz, carte de visite, Dublin, Ireland, 1916, courtesy of Kilmainham Gaol, Ireland; Fig. 12: Centre Historique des Archives Nationales, Paris, France/Bridgeman Images; Fig. 13: Artist: Hilda Dallas. Heritage Image Partnership Ltd / Alamy Stock Photo; Fig. 14: Courtesy of Drew Cameron, Combat Paper™, 2008; Fig. 15: Courtesy of Drew Cameron, Combat Paper™, 2008; Fig. 16: Ensemble, Rudi Gernreich, Resort 1970–71. Bequest of the Rudi Gernreich Estate, Courtesy of the FIDM Museum at the Fashion Institute of Design & Merchandising, Los Angeles, California; Fig. 17: Magnum Photos/Dennis Stock

Chapter 7 / Fig. 1: Hibiscus, *Luminous Procuress* film still, 1971 by Ingeborg Gerdes; Fig. 2: Photograph: Joe Mabel, GNU Free Documentation License; Fig. 3: *Leigh Bowery* by Matthew R. Lewis, 1989, resin print, 6 7/8 in. x 6 7/8 in. National Portrait Gallery, London, given by Estate of Matthew R. Lewis, 2019; Fig. 4: David Bowie and Kansai Yamamoto, © Sukita 1973. Courtesy of the photographer; Fig. 5: Harry T. Peters *America on Stone*, Lithography Collection, National Museum of American History; Fig. 6: Imageplotter News and Sports/Alamy Live News; Fig. 7: Imperial War Museum, London, IWM Non Commercial License; Fig. 8: *Una, Lady Troubridge* by Romaine Brooks, 1924, Smithsonian American Art Museum. Gift of the artist; Fig. 9: Allstar Picture Library Ltd. / Alamy Stock Photo; Fig. 10: Private Collection Photo © Christie's, Images/Bridgeman Images; Fig. 11: Florian Belmonte, 2016. Creative Commons Attribution-Share Alike 4.0 International; Fig. 12: History and Art Collection / Alamy Stock Photo; Fig. 13: *Madame Leroy* by Fabiola Jean-Louis, Rewriting History Series, 2018. Courtesy Allan Avery Gallery; Fig. 14: *Dressing for the Carnival* by Winslow Homer, 1877. Metropolitan Museum of Art,

Amelia B. Lazarus Fund, 1922; Fig. 15: Solomon Northrup by Frederick Coffin, c. 1853. Library Company of Philadelphia; Fig. 16: Yes Men Survivaball Suit, ca. 2009. Courtesy Yes Men; Fig. 17: Rachel Stine/CC0 1.0 Universal Public Domain Dedication; Fig. 18: CODEPINK Protesters, Republican National Convention, 2012. Courtesy of CODEPINK

Chapter 8 / Fig. 1: Reuters/Carlo Allegri; Fig. 2: "Speak Truth," quilt by Katherine H. McClelland, 2017. Courtesy Katherine H. McClellan; Fig. 3: Musée Carnavalet, Paris, Public Domain; Fig. 4: Public Domain; Fig. 5: Cap, wool, cotton, linen, 1790. Alfred Z. Solomon-Janet A. Sloane Endowment Fund, 2015, Metropolitan Museum of Art; Fig. 6: © Mohammed Zaanoun, Active Stills, 2019; Fig. 7: © PhotoXpress/ZUMAPRESS/ Alamy Stock Photo; Fig. 8: © Gwyn Conaway; Fig. 9: Purse, 1824–27. Helen Larson Historic Fashion Collection, FIDM Museum Purchase, funds generously donated by the Locke & Noble Tea Co. Courtesy of the FIDM Museum at the Fashion Institute of Design & Merchandising, Los Angeles, California. Photograph: Brian Sanderson; Fig. 10: mccool / Alamy Stock Photo; Fig. 11: Reuters/Andrew Burton; Fig. 12: Sarah Mason, Occupy Protester, Ted Soqui © 2011; Fig. 13: Granger Historical Picture Archive / Alamy Stock Photo; Fig. 14: Courtesy of the Commonweal Trustees and the University of Bradford, Commonweal Archives, Special Collections, 1958; Figs. 15a–15c: Courtesy of Busy Beaver Button Museum, Chicago, IL, buttonmuseum.org; Figs. 16a–16b: Birmingham Museum Picture Library. Accession number: 2001 L50.1. On loan from Gillian Smith; Fig. 17: Kanga featuring Bangladeshi activist Xulhaz Mannan by Kawira Mwirichia, 2008. Courtesy of the artist; Fig. 18: Tamiment Library Poster and Broadside Collection. Folder: United States: Native Americans; Fig. 19: Dissent Necklace by Dissent Pins/Caitlin Kuhwald. Courtesy Dissent Pins.

Chapter 9 / Fig. 1: Courtesy of Oliver Hadlee Pearch and Rudi Gernreich LLC; Fig. 2: Image © The Metropolitan Museum of Art. Image source: Art Resource, NY. Vivienne Westwood and Malcolm McLaren (British, London 1946–2010 Switzerland) (designers): "Tits" T-shirt. 1975. Cotton. Purchase, Friends of The Costume Institute; Fig. 3: © CNAC/MNAM, Dist. RMN-Grand Palais / Art Resource, NY. Export, Valie (Waltraud Höllinger) (b. 1940) © ARS, NY with Peter Hassmann (photographer). *Action Pants: Genital Panic*, 1969. Screenprint, 69.8 x 49.8 cm. Inv.: Photograph: Philippe Migeat. Musee National d'Art Moderne, Centre Georges Pompidou, Paris, France; Fig. 4: Rubin, Jerry. Joan and Robert K. Morrison Collection, 1983–1987, Archives Center, National Museum of American History; Fig. 5: Reuters/ Lucas Jackson; Fig. 6: Reuters/Stringer; Fig. 7: *Erika*, American Women of the Far Right Series by Glenna Gordon, 2017. Courtesy of

the photographer; Fig. 8: Library of Congress Archives, c. 1890s; Fig. 9: Branding, Liberation Animale 269, 2012. Courtesy Liberation Animale 269; Fig. 10: Dorothy Newell with a "suffrage plea painted on her back," in the *Topeka State Journal* (November 6, 1915). © *Chronicling America: Historic American Newspapers*, Library of Congress; Fig. 11: Photograph: In Pictures Ltd./Corbis via Getty Images; Fig. 12: Associated Press; Fig. 13: Reuters/Arko Datta (INDIA). Alamy Stock Photo; Fig. 14: Bruce Davidson, Magnum Photos; Fig. 15: *Runner Rosalie Fish with red handprint over face to represent Murdered and Missing Indigenous Women*, horizontal, color taken by *The Spokesman-Review*, May 25, 2019. Tyler Tjomsland / THE SPOKESMAN-REVIEW; Fig. 16: Dennis Rodman, "Naked" Campaign, PETA, 1990–2020. Courtesy People for the Ethical Treatment of Animals (PETA); Fig. 17: Kiran Gandhi, 2015 London Marathon, England. Courtesy Kiran Gandhi; Fig. 18: Anima Naturalis Protesters, Barcelona, Spain, December 7, 2015. Courtesy of Anima Naturalis

Conclusion / Fig. 1: Reuters/TT News Agency; Fig. 2: Reuters/Andrew Kelly; Fig. 3: Reuters/ Jonathan Drake; Fig. 4: Sky Cubacub, Rebirth Garments. Photographer: Colectivo Multipolar @colectivomultipolar; Fig. 5: Reuters/Lucas Jackson

Index